THE GIRL WHO FOUGHT BACK

Vladka Meed **and the Warsaw Ghetto Uprising**

Also by Joshua M. Greene

Signs of Survival: A Memoir of the Holocaust

Cowritten with Renee Hartman

My Survival: A Girl on Schindler's List

Cowritten with Rena Finder

THE GIRL WHO FOUGHT BACK

Vladka Meed and the Warsaw Ghetto Uprising

JOSHUA M. GREENE

Scholastic Focus ▪ New York

Library of Congress Cataloging-in-Publication Data

Names: Greene, Joshua, 1950– author.
Title: The girl who fought back : Vladka Meed and the Warsaw Ghetto Uprising / Joshua M. Greene.
Other titles: Vladka Meed and the Warsaw Ghetto Uprising
Description: First edition. | New York : Scholastic Focus, 2024. | Audience: Ages 9–12 | Audience: Grades 7–9 | Summary: "Warsaw, Poland, 1940s: The Nazis are on the march, determined to wipe out the Jewish people of Europe. Teenage Vladka and her family are among the thousands of Jews forced to relocate behind the walls of the Warsaw Ghetto, a cramped, oppressive space full of starvation, suffering, and death. When Vladka's family is deported to concentration camps, Vladka joins up with other young people in the ghetto who are part of the Jewish underground: a group determined to fight back against the Nazis, no matter the cost. Vladka's role in the underground? To pass as a non-Jew, sneaking out of the ghetto to blend into Polish society while smuggling secret messages and weapons back over the ghetto wall. Every move she makes comes with the risk of being arrested or killed. But Vladka and her friends know that their missions are worth the danger—they are preparing for an uprising like no other, one that will challenge the Nazi war machine. This astonishing true story of the Warsaw Ghetto Uprising, told through the lens of Holocaust survivor and educator Vladka Meed, introduces readers to a crucial piece of history while highlighting the persistence of bravery in the face of hate"— Provided by publisher.
Identifiers: LCCN 2023015950 | ISBN 9781338880519 (hardback) | ISBN 9781338880540 (ebook)
Subjects: LCSH: Miedzyrzecki, Feigele Peltel—Juvenile literature. | Jewish teenagers—Poland—Warsaw—Biography—Juvenile literature. | Warsaw (Poland)—History—Warsaw Ghetto Uprising, 1943—Juvenile literature. | World War, 1939–1945—Underground movements—Poland—Juvenile literature. | Żydowska Organizacja Bojowa (Poland)—Juvenile literature. | Holocaust, Jewish (1939–1945)—Poland—Warsaw—Biography—Juvenile literature. | Jews—Poland—Warsaw—Biography—Juvenile literature. | Holocaust survivors—Biography—Juvenile literature. | BISAC: JUVENILE NONFICTION / Biography & Autobiography / Historical | JUVENILE NONFICTION / Family / General (see also headings under Social Topics)
Classification: LCC DS134.72.M54 G74 2024 | DDC 940.53/1853841—dc23/eng/20230603
LC record available at https://lccn.loc.gov/2023015950

To the Warsaw Ghetto fighters,
all of whom deserve to be remembered.

THE GIRL WHO FOUGHT BACK

Vladka Meed **and the Warsaw Ghetto Uprising**

INTRODUCTION

The Warsaw Ghetto Uprising was one of the most important events in modern history. Over the course of about four weeks in 1943, seven hundred and fifty Jewish women and men—most of them teenagers with no military training—held off the powerful Nazi army using only a handful of weapons. Never in Germany's campaign to conquer Europe and exterminate the Jewish population had their forces encountered such resistance.

But the uprising was also an act of desperation. The young Jewish fighters in the ghetto knew the Nazis were committed to murdering every Jew in Poland. The resisters did not expect to survive.

This book tells the story of Vladka Meed, one of the few resisters who did survive the Warsaw Ghetto Uprising. Her story is retold from a variety of sources, including video recordings she made between 1946 and 2012, a memoir she wrote after the end of World War II, and memoirs by other survivors of the uprising, including a video interview with her husband, Ben Meed. Additional historical details have been added for clarity, but the story is completely hers.

Read on, and be inspired by what one young woman and her friends were able to do against an entire army.

WORLD WAR II

World War II, or the Second World War, lasted from 1939 to 1945. It was by far the deadliest conflict in human history, resulting in the deaths of 70 to 85 million people, including both combatants and civilians.

World War II pitted the Allied countries—principally Britain, the Soviet Union, and the United States of America—against the Axis powers: Nazi Germany, Fascist Italy, and Imperial Japan.

World War II is generally considered to have begun on September 1, 1939, when Nazi Germany, under its dictator, Adolf Hitler, invaded Poland. Two days later, Britain and France responded by declaring war on Germany. Within a year, Germany had defeated France and conquered the Netherlands, Belgium, Luxembourg, Norway, and Denmark. Wherever Germany conquered territory, it targeted local Jewish populations with massacres and deportations to death camps as part of a campaign of genocide now known as the Holocaust.

On June 22, 1941, Germany invaded the Soviet Union (today Russia) but was pushed back by overwhelming Soviet forces and brutal winter conditions. The war in Europe concluded with the liberation of German-occupied territories by the Allied forces, culminating in Hitler's suicide and Germany's surrender on May 8, 1945.

PREFACE

The Warsaw ghetto was burning.

A ten-foot-high brick wall separated the ghetto from the rest of the city. From where she stood, on the street outside the ghetto, Vladka could see buildings consumed by flames.

The ghetto had been burning for six days now, forcing Jews out of their hiding places in attics and cellars. Vladka saw families huddled together on the ghetto rooftops, cornered by flames. The fire came closer, and the families jumped.

Vladka closed her eyes. She knew those people, the ones who were dying.

There came the loud *whoosh* of gasoline-powered flamethrowers. The Nazi soldiers were destroying the ghetto, building by building. Vladka heard the *rat-a-tat-tat* of German machine guns as the Nazis murdered everyone who had run out onto the streets of the ghetto to escape the burning buildings.

It was the Christian holiday of Palm Sunday, and on Vladka's side of the wall, parents were coming out of church services with their children. Not far from where she stood was a merry-go-round. Parents lifted their children up onto wooden horses and clapped, watching them ride gaily round and round while a steam organ with tall pipes played circus music.

The parents knew the ghetto was burning. They could see the same flames Vladka saw leaping into the sky. They could hear the same machine guns and smell the same smoke. They could even feel the intense heat, but they were busy enjoying a spring day with their children and had no time or pity for dying Jews. Vladka heard one parent say to another, as he calmly pointed to the flames raging on the other side of the wall, "Look at that. The Jews are frying today."

Vladka said nothing. What choice did she have? She was one of fifty or so young people working undercover outside the ghetto wall. Maintaining her cover was crucial to the mission of sabotaging the Nazis' efforts.

Less than three years earlier, the Nazis had forced all the Jews of Warsaw to move into the ghetto. Vladka had been among them. Since then, Vladka and fellow members of the resistance, most of them between the ages of fifteen and thirty, had told themselves that one day they would fight back. They would confront the Nazis in the open. Now Vladka could hear her friends fighting back, and she understood that moment had come.

If Vladka and her friends were going to die, they would die fighting.

1943—Apartment buildings burning during the
Nazi suppression of the Warsaw Ghetto Uprising.

Chapter 1

IN DISGUISE

Four years earlier, on a warm November evening, a teenager named Feige Peltel—whom we will call by her code name, Vladka—hurried down the city street with a tray of sewing supplies. If she was lucky, she might sell all the colorful ribbons, zippers, fasteners, and spools of thread, and make it home before dark. She was headed to Warsaw's wealthier section, where people had money to spend.

This was Vladka's first attempt at disguising herself. She had put on makeup and was wearing her best dress. With her light-brown hair and gray-green eyes, Vladka looked how a non-Jew was thought to look. Unlike most Jews whose first language was Yiddish, Vladka spoke fluent Polish, which counted for a lot when pretending to be a Christian. Naturally, she had taken off the white armband with the blue star that all Jews were required to wear. If people found out that she was a Jew trying to do business with non-Jews, the police would be summoned, and she would be carted off to jail.

Vladka reminded herself to stay calm while streetcars drove by with the familiar *clang-clang* of traffic bells. The streets were filled with cars, trucks, horse-drawn carts, and bicycles. Vladka dodged the traffic, impatient to get to Saski Park before it got too late. Even non-Jews could be arrested for staying out past the 7 p.m. curfew.

It was November 1939. Germany had invaded Poland two months before, and Vladka thought about how different things were now. Warsaw had once been the largest center of Jewish life in all of Eastern Europe. Theaters put on plays in Yiddish, and movie houses showed films featuring Jewish actors. The city was home to Jewish publishing companies, sports clubs, and cultural centers, and Jewish businesses thrived. Jews made up almost 30 percent of the city's 1.1 million residents, including many of Poland's most respected doctors, lawyers, educators, writers, and artists. Vladka's family wasn't rich, but she had many friends, and she loved attending cultural and artistic events. Her life was good.

That all changed when Nazi Germany invaded, and an unending series of edicts restricted the lives of Polish Jews. Vladka and her family, like all the other Jews in Warsaw, were forced to surrender their bicycles, radios, and any other valuables they possessed. Vladka knew many Jews whose businesses were taken away by the Nazis and given to non-Jews. Jewish people were not allowed to shop outside specific hours. The Nazis also forbade Jewish children from attending school, so Vladka had stopped going.

Vladka didn't know this yet, but soon Jews would be forbidden to use the railways without special permission. Next would come decrees that forbade Jews from entering restaurants and public parks. By the fall of 1940, the German authorities would conscript more than 100,000 Jewish men, women, and children into slave labor, forcing them to clear away piles of garbage and debris from the city streets and work in factories that made weapons and other supplies for the German army. The Jews received no pay for this labor, the hours were long, and their Nazi bosses didn't hesitate to use whips and clubs to make them work harder.

What Vladka *did* know was that her non-Jewish friends had changed, almost overnight. Her Christian neighbors and schoolmates, once kind to her, had become fiercely antisemitic, ready to report to the police any Jews who tried to hide their identity. The Nazis had unleashed something dark and cruel in the people around her, turning friends into enemies.

Vladka finally arrived at Saski Park and politely approached people sitting on benches. With a bright smile and speaking impeccable Polish, she described the various sewing supplies she was selling. Around her, handsomely dressed couples strolled arm in arm on their way to dinner or a show. Herons and ducks from the nearby Vistula River flew overhead. *Perhaps they are heading south for the winter,* Vladka thought. She looked past the park at the skyline of the city and admired the intricately carved Gothic buildings that rose from the ruins of other buildings, the ones that had been destroyed by Nazi bombs during the invasion.

Warsaw is still such a beautiful city, she told herself.

There was no way she could have known that, by the end of World War II, 90 percent of everything around her would be razed to the ground. Most of the city would be reduced to rubble. By then, too, most of her friends in the underground would be dead.

After selling as many sewing supplies as she could, Vladka took a trolley back to her family's apartment in the suburb of Praga. At home, she found her parents and younger siblings—her sister, Henia, and brother, Chaim—listening to the radio. Vladka recognized the voice of Adolf Hitler, chancellor of Germany and head of the Nazi Party.

Hitler was shouting another one of his tirades against Jews, something about how Jews were not human, that they were bacteria that had to be removed before they could contaminate German society.

Vladka was disgusted and frightened by Hitler's strong rhetoric, but her father, Shlomo, told her not to worry.

"I knew many Germans when I was a soldier in the First World War," he said. "They're good people. They won't treat us the way Hitler is telling them to."

Vladka loved her father very much. He was a good man, handsome, with blue eyes and gray hair, and he was respected by their friends for his learning. But Vladka knew he was a bit of a dreamer and naive about what the Nazis were capable of doing to Jews.

In Vladka's opinion, her mother, Hanna, was the more practical parent. It was Hanna who kept the apartment clean and ran their small haberdashery store that sold hats, gloves, scarves, and sewing supplies. Vladka's mother was optimistic by nature, and very resourceful. She could make meals from a handful of potatoes and a little flour. Ever since the Nazi occupation, it had become almost impossible for Jews to find someone willing to sell them food. Yet Hanna somehow managed to find enough food to feed the family.

Each morning, Vladka's thirteen-year-old brother, Chaim, ran several blocks to the spot where bread rations were handed out. German officials had authorized distribution of bread to the citizens of Warsaw, but only to the Christians. Jews were excluded, yet Chaim took the risk of standing in line for his family every day.

Unlike Vladka, Chaim had what the Nazis considered to be stereotypical "Jewish features," including a prominent nose, dark-brown hair, and dark-brown eyes. One morning, a man on the bread line pointed at him and yelled, "Look, there's a Jew!" Soldiers ran over and beat Chaim with clubs. He managed to escape before they could do worse.

Vladka handed her mother the money she had earned in Saski Park, and a thought came to her: Looking like a Gentile could be useful. She had gotten away with pretending not to be Jewish this one time—maybe she could get away with it again.

NAZI RACISM

The Nazis invented a description of an ideal human: blond, blue-eyed, athletic, tall, strong, and Christian. They called these ideal persons "Aryans," even though many Germans did not fit the description. Adolf Hitler himself had brown hair and was average height.

Nonetheless, the Nazis believed that Germans were the "master race" and should be protected from infection by "inferior" races, Jews in particular. In 1935, the Germans passed racial laws—called the Nuremberg Laws—that defined a Jew as anyone who was born Jewish, who had three grandparents who were Jews, or anyone who believed in the Jewish faith. Even Jews who had converted to Christianity were still considered Jews under these laws.

Students in Nazi-run schools were taught *Rassenkunde*, Nazi racial theory, which considered a person's genetic history and physical features in determining their racial "purity." Jewish "impurities" included a pronounced nose and skull, dark eyes, and dark hair. The Nazis pointed to these and other fabricated "impurities" to encourage the non-Jews of Germany to hate Jews and other minorities.

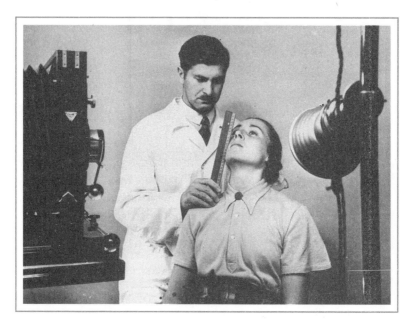

1930s—A Nazi teacher measures a German student's nose in a class on *Rassenkunde*, Nazi racial theory.

Chapter 2

THE GHETTO

Ever since the German invasion, Vladka heard rumors that the Jews of Warsaw would be forced to move into a ghetto. In the summer of 1940, the rumors proved true: German officials forced teams of Jewish workers to build a ten-foot-high brick wall around a designated area of 1.3 square miles. This small, enclosed area was to be the Jewish ghetto. Construction of the wall was completed in November, and all the Jews of Warsaw were ordered to leave their homes and relocate inside the ghetto.

Vladka, her parents, and her siblings piled their belongings onto a hand-pulled wooden wagon and walked down the city's cobblestone streets. Progress was difficult; all around them, hundreds of thousands of Jewish men, women, and children were making the same journey to the ghetto.

Vladka and her family arrived at the brick wall that separated the ghetto from the rest of the world and wheeled their belongings past the wooden barricade.

There had already been Jewish families living inside the Jewish quarter that was now isolated behind the ghetto wall. With so many more families forced to relocate there, the small area became unbearably crowded.

Vladka and her family went looking for a place to stay in the ghetto. The best they could find was a tiny apartment on the third floor of a crumbling building. Vladka thought back to their comfortable three-bedroom apartment. Now she, her parents, and her siblings would be sharing one room and a filthy kitchen, so drenched with moisture from leaking water that she could write her name on the wall with her finger.

Vladka exchanged looks with her family. They knew things were only going to get worse and feared that, eventually, the Germans would kill them. They just didn't know when or how. For the moment, the family's main concern was making enough money to buy food.

Vladka left the tiny apartment and wandered the streets of the ghetto, searching for an opportunity to earn some money. She saw tables and chairs lining the sidewalks that displayed shoes, shirts, socks, pots, pans, mirrors, cups, and plates. Some people were selling cups of coffee. Others hung belongings from their windows, including bedsheets, blankets, and winter coats. Children had set up displays of toys and candies—anything at all that might bring in money for food. Whatever the Jews of the ghetto owned, they were willing to sell.

Vladka noticed that Germans guarding the entrance to the ghetto were allowing non-Jews from outside to come in and shop. *Since the Jews are selling everything they own*, the Polish Gentiles must have thought, *why not take advantage of their misfortune and buy goods at a bargain price?*

As she walked on, Vladka peered inside entrances to buildings, and she shuddered. In almost every doorway, she saw people young and old, emaciated and dying of starvation.

When she returned to the tiny apartment, her family swapped reports of the day's activities. Vladka's father had tried to sell some cloth from the shop they once ran, but German police robbed him of the goods and beat him up. Vladka's sister, Henia, had found work in a public soup kitchen. Chaim was too young to work. He would stay home to help their mother with the cooking and cleaning. Vladka explained that she had found a job as a cashier in a barbershop. It paid next to nothing, but every little bit helped.

Even with everyone trying their best, there was barely any money and very little to eat. Shlomo was constantly depressed over their situation, and as the weeks went by, Vladka watched her father slowly fade away. He grew sick from pneumonia and hunger. It was impossible to get any medicine, and his depression only worsened his condition. Shlomo was the kind of person who could not live with the shame of failing to provide for his family.

One day, he turned his head to the wall, closed his eyes, and died.

That was the first time Vladka witnessed death up close. It would not be the last.

THE WARSAW GHETTO

As an interim step between persecuting Jews and killing them, the Nazis forced the Jews of Europe to move into congested slums called ghettos. There were more than one thousand ghettos in Nazi-occupied countries across Europe. The largest was the Warsaw ghetto, which housed nearly a half-million people—30 percent of the city's population compressed into only one square mile of buildings. Inside the ghetto, Nazi soldiers terrorized Jews. They helped themselves to anything of value that the Jews possessed, beat them with clubs, and shot them.

Starvation was part of the Nazi strategy for eliminating the Jews of Europe. The official daily quota of food for Jews in the ghetto was only 400 calories, the equivalent of two slices of bread and a little butter. Later, the Nazis reduced it to 200 calories per day. No one could live on so little, and ghetto residents supplemented the starvation diet by smuggling in food from outside the ghetto. Much of the smuggling was done by children small enough to squeeze in and out of sewers and other openings in the brick wall.

Very few people in the ghetto had any income. Trading was a common means of getting food, but there was little food available even for people with something to trade, and the death rate from starvation and lack of medical care spiraled. Between October 1940 and July 1942, when deportations began, more than 90,000 residents died—nearly 20 percent of the entire population of the ghetto.

1941—Shopping and bartering in a Warsaw ghetto street market.

Chapter 3

TAKEN AWAY

For two years, while struggling to survive inside the ghetto, Vladka and her family heard reports of deportations.

The reports described German soldiers storming into the homes of Jews without any warning, rounding them up, and sending them by train to concentration camps, where they were tortured and killed.

Still, even in the spring of 1942, such reports seemed little more than rumors.

By July 1942, Vladka had moved into a tiny room in a separate apartment. One morning, Vladka heard a commotion in the street below her window. She rushed down the stairs and elbowed her way through a crowd of people. They were all gasping and moaning over announcements that had been posted on the walls so recently that the ink on the paper was still wet.

By order of the German authorities, all the Jews
of Warsaw, regardless of age or sex, are to be
deported. Only those employed in the German
workshops, the Jewish community council, the
Jewish police department, and the Jewish hospital
will be exempt. Every deportee will be permitted to
carry no more than fifteen kilograms of luggage,
including cash, valuables, and provisions to last
three days. Those failing to comply with this edict
will be subject to the death penalty.

Vladka stared in horror. *So, it's true*, she thought. *The next*
phase of the Nazis' plan to murder us has begun.

Her sister was still working in the soup kitchen, and
Vladka now had a job as a seamstress in the Toebbens
sewing factory, which made clothes for the German army.
Because Vladka and her sister had these "approved" jobs,
for the moment they were safe from deportation.

Her mother and brother, however, did not have approved
jobs, which were few and hard to get. Vladka heard that
some people bribed their way into an approved job while
others purchased forged work papers. But either of those

options would cost a small fortune, and her family had no money.

Vladka noticed that, within a day of the deportation announcement, the poor and sick disappeared from the streets of the ghetto. They knew they were of no use to the Germans and would be the first ones sent to their deaths, so they had gone into hiding.

The only solution was for Vladka's mother and brother to do the same.

The best places to hide were in lofts, cellars, or tiny spaces behind walls or under floors. One night, when the ghetto's streets were empty, Vladka brought her mother and brother to the soup kitchen where her sister worked and hid them in the cellar. She knew they would not be able to stay there very long—people were coming and going from the soup kitchen all the time—but it might work for a few days.

The alternative was do nothing and wait for the Germans to deport them, but that was too painful to imagine. Vladka had heard terrible stories about the concentration camp Treblinka, where the Germans sent most of the Jews from Warsaw. These reports from prisoners who had escaped and returned to the ghetto haunted her at night.

Vladka had hidden her mother and brother just in time: deportations began the next day. That morning, as Vladka left her apartment to go to her job at the sewing factory, she saw army trucks pull up on her street. German soldiers jumped out and stopped people at random. They pushed anyone without valid work papers into the trucks. Anyone who tried to resist was immediately shot.

A few nights after the deportation, when Vladka felt it was safe, she collected her mother and brother from the cellar and hurried them back to their apartment. Then she returned to the small room where she lived.

The following morning, she was awakened by gunfire in the street below. She heard the crash of falling glass and people screaming. There were heavy footsteps on the stairs of her building and a loud banging on her door. She knew it was another deportation by the Germans.

"Downstairs!" a man's voice yelled out. "Everyone! Be quick about it!"

Vladka threw on some clothes, grabbed her work permit, and hurried downstairs.

In the street, she was surrounded by people running and pushing, everyone holding on tightly to suitcases and bundles of clothing. Parents and children were clinging to one another. She saw grown-ups pleading with police to let their families stay together. The officers consulted papers listing who lived in which buildings and shouted out their names. Vladka was caught up in the rush, pushed this way and that while looking frantically around her. Where were her mother and brother? Had they been taken? She knew her sister, Henia, was at work, so at least she was safe, for now.

"Have your work papers ready for inspection!"

Vladka watched German soldiers and Jewish police examine people's papers and order them to either the right side or the left side of the street. Those sent to the right were the lucky ones who had valid work permits and would be allowed to go home. The unlucky ones, those without work permits, were sent to the left side of the street to await deportation.

Vladka noticed that for many, even having a work permit meant nothing. If a soldier didn't like the way someone looked, that was sufficient reason for the soldier to kill him. She watched an old man, bent over with age, approach a soldier and show him his papers. The soldier pushed the man's hand away and hit him hard on the head with the butt of his rifle. The old man staggered and fell to the ground.

Vladka felt herself losing hope. *What has become of us?* she wondered. *We're nothing but objects, forced to do whatever the Nazis order us to do. What difference does it make if I live or die? Whatever is going to happen, let it happen. I just want this to be over.*

She scanned the crowd on the opposite side of the street, hoping to not see her mother or brother among those awaiting deportation. Officers with drawn pistols were pushing the condemned onto trucks and streetcars that would take them to the train station. Vladka thought she heard her brother's voice calling from one of the streetcars, but she couldn't be sure. Everyone around her was screaming out the names of relatives, and it was hard to hear anything clearly.

Hours later, the sun was setting, but many who had been caught in the roundup were still waiting to be processed. Vladka recognized a man named Julian Welikowski and his wife and child. Before the Nazi occupation, Julian had been Vladka's teacher in public school. In the last few years, Vladka had seen him work day and night to organize classes for children in the ghetto. Now she watched as he showed his family's papers to one of the German officers. The officer looked at him and, noting with disapproval his glasses and scholarly demeanor, waved the papers aside.

"Left!" he ordered, sending the teacher and his family to their death.

She watched another neighbor present his family's documents.

"Man to the right!" the policeman ordered. "Wife and child to the left!"

The man pleaded with the policeman to not separate them. The policeman nodded in agreement—and pushed the whole family to the left for deportation.

When Vladka's turn came, she showed the officer a note that authorized her to work at the Toebbens clothing factory. Everyone knew Toebbens. It was the largest German workshop in the ghetto.

"How do I know this is a valid work card?" the officer demanded.

"Look," she said, pointing. "There's my name. I'm a seamstress in the Toebbens factory."

"To the right!" he yelled, then shoved Vladka in with the "safe" ones.

One by one, the trucks and streetcars departed. After a few minutes, the street was empty and quiet. Vladka watched soldiers sidestep bodies, rip open abandoned suitcases and pocket money, silverware, and anything else of value.

Around her were the corpses of Jews who had been shot or beaten. She looked up and saw others who like her had been spared thanks to their work permits. No one said a thing. They all stared in the direction where their families had been taken away.

Then she heard someone say, "At least the rest of us have been spared."

A question that had been simmering inside her for weeks boiled over. *There are only a few Nazi soldiers and several thousand of us. Why has no one, including me, done anything? We're all going to die anyway. Why don't we fight back?*

There were no answers, no more screams, just a growing awareness for Vladka that the total destruction of the Jewish people had begun. Due to luck or chance or some reason only God understood, she, from tens of thousands who had been processed that day, was among the small handful still alive.

Now she had to find out if her mother and brother had somehow survived as well.

DEPORTATIONS

In March 1942, as part of a plan to systematically murder all Jews in German-occupied Poland, the Nazis began deporting people by train from the Warsaw ghetto to concentration camps. By the end of 1942, more than two million of Poland's three million Jews had been murdered in the camps. During the next two years, the ghettos were completely liquidated, and their inhabitants were either shot and buried in mass graves or else transported by trains and trucks to extermination camps.

There were six such extermination camps, also called death camps. The Germans sent most of the Jews from Warsaw to a death camp called Treblinka. Deportees arriving there were immediately murdered, and by the end of the war in 1945, the Nazis and their allies had murdered more than six million Jewish men, women, and children.

July 1942—Nazi officers force Jews from the
Warsaw ghetto to board a deportation train.

Chapter 4

A FAMILY LOST

Vladka hurried to her mother's building. She raced up the stairs, terrified that she might find the apartment empty, which would mean her mother and brother had been deported.

Her worst fears were confirmed. There was no one there, only a half-spilled bag of cornmeal on the kitchen table next to a bowl of water.

She must have been making dumplings for my brother when the deportations began, Vladka thought. *Too bad they never had a chance to eat them. They must have been very hungry . . .*

Vladka held her face in her hands and wept. She knew she would never see her mother or brother again. In all likelihood, they would be murdered by the Nazis, just like others who had been deported, including so many of her friends, neighbors, teachers, and classmates.

What was she supposed to do now? Just go on working like a slave for the Germans by day and scrounging for a mouthful of food by night? She was young and healthy. She was smart. Her looks allowed her to pass as a non-Jew. She could take risks others couldn't. But doing what?

Before the war, when she still attended school, Vladka had been encouraged by her parents to be socially active. She joined several youth groups, including the youth division of the Labor Bund, Warsaw's largest Jewish party. The Bund was concerned with creating a more socially and economically equitable environment for everyone—a policy referred to as "democratic socialism." Vladka became a leader among her Bund friends.

After the deportation of her mother and brother, Vladka found comfort in the company of young people in the ghetto, many of whom had been her friends in the Bund. Together, these young people joined the "underground." These were groups working to help other Jews in secret, under the direction of an umbrella group called the Jewish Fighting Organization—known in Polish as the *Żydowska Organizacja Bojowa*, or the ŻOB for short.

At first, Vladka and her friends organized illegal classes that taught Jews where to find food or clothing or information about missing loved ones. Eventually, their duties would become more and more dangerous.

In the meantime, Vladka knew that her job at the Toebbens factory would keep her fairly safe from deportation. Her sister, Henia, though, was not so lucky. Vladka received word that her sister's kitchen was to be closed. When Vladka learned Henia's job no longer offered protection from deportation, she rushed to warn her.

"Come back to my place right now," Vladka pleaded. "We're all that's left of our family, and we must stick together."

"I can't," Henia said. "This kitchen feeds children. How can I abandon the children? Besides, even the Germans wouldn't stop us from doing such important work."

Vladka returned home, angry at herself for failing to convince her sister to leave and terrified over what might happen to Henia. The next day, Vladka learned that the rumors had been true. The Germans raided the kitchen and loaded the entire staff onto wagons for deportation to Treblinka. Henia was among them.

Vladka never saw her sister again.

Chapter 5

IN THE FACTORY

Each day, Vladka went to work consumed by grief and regret over the loss of her family. Why had she not also been deported? Why was she still alive and not them?

Some of Vladka's friends in the ŻOB—the underground— also had work permits for the Toebbens factory, and every morning they walked there together. The factory was located in a four-story building that had once been a Jewish hospital. Along the way, Vladka and her friends were obliged to step carefully over broken furniture, abandoned suitcases, and the bodies of murdered Jewish men, women, and children.

Once in the building, Vladka joined a crowd of other workers in an enormous room full of sewing machines and tables loaded with bolts of cloth and boxes of fittings. For the next twelve hours, they cut and sewed cloth, stitched buttonholes, and assembled thousands of uniforms and other garments for the German army. Vladka ran her hands back and forth under the sewing machine until her eyes watered and her fingers ached.

When Vladka had first started working there, the factory was still in the final stages of construction. She and the other workers spent their time carrying in sewing machines and installing benches, cutting tables, and chairs. Everyone was anxious to start making clothes and demonstrate to their German supervisor that they were productive workers, worth keeping alive.

Once the sewing part of her job started, Vladka was relieved. The work was familiar to her; she'd learned how to sew from her mother, a very talented seamstress. There were different sizes of uniforms and jackets to be made, each with its particular pieces of cloth. An experienced seamstress, such as Vladka, knew how to cut the cloth into precise shapes, how to match the pieces together, and which stitching to use for making a jacket or pants strong enough to last under wartime conditions.

Only a few of the other workers, she noticed, could do that as well. Hundreds of people had applied for a job in the clothing factory, but most had little or no experience making clothes. They'd applied out of fear for their lives, desperate for a job, and had lied about their skills. The older people were the most desperate, since they were the Jews least useful to the Germans and the most likely to be deported.

One morning, Vladka had barely begun sewing when someone burst in and announced that Germans were on their way up the stairs. Another roundup was happening.

There was little actual work to do in the factory that day, as fabric for uniforms was in short supply. Workers quickly picked up whatever pieces of cloth they could find lying around the factory floor and ran them through their sewing machines, inventing tasks and hoping the Germans would see how industrious they were and let them live. Mothers who had brought their children to the factory looked frantically for places to hide them.

The door to the workshop slammed open and officers stormed into the room.

"Everyone here must be an authorized worker!" they yelled. "And you better not be hiding any children!"

The Nazis searched under tables and inside closets and arrested children, old people, and anyone else they didn't like and marched them away. Vladka and the other remaining workers dared not say a word but continued cutting and sewing as though nothing had happened.

After the factory closed for the day, Vladka was too shaken to go home. She walked with other young workers to the apartment of Manya Wasser, the wife of a ŻOB leader. There were rumors of yet another roundup that night, and Manya had invited them to stay with her. The dozen or so young people filed quietly into the small apartment. No one said a word. They sat in a circle around a small lamp and listened in fear for the stomping of German boots coming up the stairs to arrest them.

Manya's sister, Roma, who had been a teacher before the ghetto, was the first to break the silence.

"I'd like to tell you about a trip I once took to Vienna," she said.

Vladka noticed that Roma seemed calm and even smiled a little. That was odd. How could anyone be calm at a time like this? And why would she want to talk about some vacation she took when they could be deported at any moment and sent to their deaths?

Roma described how impressed she'd been by Vienna's elegant cafés, beautiful parks, and museums, and how friendly everyone was—

"That's enough," a young man spoke up. "Vienna is the capital of Nazi Austria. How can you talk about those people at a time like this? Are any of your 'friendly' Austrians coming to help us?"

He's right, Vladka thought, and a heated discussion followed. Several of the friends expressed anger at the world for ignoring their tragic situation. Roma disagreed.

"Do you think the whole world is as cruel and bloodthirsty as the Nazis are?" she asked. "Or that the whole world even knows what goes on here and has chosen to do nothing?"

Vladka did not take part in the discussion. She hated arguing, and besides, her own losses were still too fresh. Still, she admired Roma's faith in people, especially when there were millions of Nazis who wanted Hitler to succeed and every Jew to die. There followed a discussion about human nature that continued all night, and for those few hours Vladka and her friends had something other than their sorrowful fates to think about.

A few days later, the Germans conducted a roundup on Roma's street. Roma was arrested and deported to the Treblinka death camp.

Vladka never saw her again.

Circa 1942—Jews working in the Warsaw ghetto branch
of the Toebbens factory, making Nazi uniforms, socks,
and other articles of clothing for the German army.

THE CAMPS

The Germans established more than 44,000 camps for the enslavement, forced labor, torture, starvation, and murder of anyone the Nazi regime deemed "undesirable." The system of camps was an integral part of the Nazis' campaign to exterminate Europe's Jews.

Concentration camps were specifically for the detention of civilians whom the Nazis considered "enemies of the state," such as political prisoners, Roma ("gypsies" was the pejorative term used at the time), Jehovah's Witnesses, gay people and others accused of "antisocial" behavior, and above all Jews.

Some camps were primarily for forced labor, where prisoners were made to work twelve hours a day or more, laying roads, digging ditches, or manufacturing weapons and supplies. Although labor camps were not overtly meant to kill prisoners, hundreds of thousands still died from ill-treatment, disease, and starvation.

Transit camps were temporary holding facilities for Jews awaiting deportation to more permanent camps such as Bergen-Belsen or Auschwitz.

Killing centers such as Treblinka were for the assembly-line murder of large numbers of people immediately upon arrival. Nearly a million people, mostly Jews, were killed at Treblinka during the eighteen months of its operation.

Some camps changed status over time. Auschwitz, the largest of all camps, began as a detention center after Germany's invasion of Poland in 1939. By the spring of 1942, Jews arriving at Auschwitz were immediately gassed to death, and the camp became a death camp in its true sense.

Chapter 6

A CASUAL KILLING

In the ghetto, Vladka now shared a tiny, cold, rundown apartment with four other young people from the underground.

One was a young man named Yankel Gruszka, who held classes for children and was loved for his kindness and devotion. Then there was a young woman named Edzia Russ, who had been Vladka's schoolmate when they were younger, and who was determined to resist any feelings of despair. There was Edzia's husband, Henach, the tall leader of their little group who had blazing eyes and a reassuring smile. And there was Shlomo Pav, who had once been a cheerful young man. After his wife was deported, Shlomo became depressed, wandered aimlessly around the tiny apartment, and kept mostly to himself. The five friends shared their sufferings and helped one another fight hunger, exhaustion, and loss of hope over their fate at the hands of the Nazis.

Their apartment had two small rooms with a door in between, which was hidden behind a freestanding wooden closet. At the back of the closet, they cut an opening. In an emergency, they could crawl through from one room to the other and hide.

One morning in September 1942, the Germans posted an announcement ordering all Jews still in the ghetto—meaning the lucky ones who still had work permits—to trade in their old permits for new ones. The old permits, they declared, were no longer valid. The Germans knew that many Jews were using forged permits, and issuing new ones was an effective way to round up more people to kill.

Vladka, along with her friends Edzia and Henach, went to the office in the ghetto where the new work permits were being handed out. The office overflowed with people jostling for a good position at the front of the line, hoping to be first to receive the new permits. An officer from the Jewish police used his baton to push people back. Women combed their hair and smiled, hoping to convince the officer they were healthy and therefore good workers.

Vladka spotted a familiar face, and her blood ran cold. It was the German supervisor from the Toebbens factory. In the factory, nothing escaped the glare of this supervisor, who carried a leather riding crop and kept everyone working long and hard. Vladka and her fellow workers were often exhausted, their eyes burning from so many hours of sewing, and their stomachs growling from hunger. They couldn't wait for the end of their shift when they would get a tiny ration of thin soup and then be allowed to go home to sleep.

Sometimes even this little bit of relief was denied, like when the supervisor received a bigger than usual order for uniforms. At such times, he forced his crews to work two days or more without stopping. If anyone put their head down from exhaustion even for a moment, the supervisor's riding crop came crashing down on their back.

In the room where Vladka sewed, workers used a wooden closet as a hiding place and took turns resting inside for a half hour or so. One day, the German supervisor opened the closet door and found sixteen-year-old Raisel, the youngest sewing machine operator, asleep. The supervisor beat her mercilessly with his riding crop. His face was red with anger, and he foamed at the mouth. Vladka watched but could say nothing.

As soon as he left, Vladka rushed to help Raisel, who was bruised and bleeding. Then the workers heard screams and groans from other rooms. Clearly, the supervisor had not stopped his beatings with Raisel.

In the office where the new permits were being handed out, Vladka stood at attention while the German supervisor walked back and forth, slapping the new permits against the palm of his hand, as if deciding who deserved one and who didn't. He stopped in front of Vladka and her comrades, who all held out their hands. To their great relief, the supervisor gave them all new permits. They could now go back to work. They were safe—but for how long? Like every other Jew in the ghetto, Vladka knew death waited for her around every corner. She stared at the permit, which guaranteed nothing, and cried.

Her comrades put their arms around her and together they walked back to the Toebbens factory. A policeman guarded the street leading to the factory entrance. They showed him their new work permits and he waved them through. Across the street, Vladka noticed an old woman walking alone, taking short, slow steps. At that moment, a German army vehicle pulled up alongside the old woman, and a soldier in the front seat called out for her to stop.

The old woman continued plodding along as though she had not heard him.

Perhaps she's deaf, Vladka thought. *Or maybe she's just dizzy from the heat of the day. It's warm for this time of year.*

The soldier climbed casually out of his car, walked up to the old woman, drew his gun, and shot her. The woman collapsed dead on the ground. The soldier climbed back into his vehicle and drove off.

Vladka and her friends were in shock, but they had no choice other than continuing on to the factory.

Once seated at her workstation, Vladka tried to make sense of what she had just seen. Had human beings fallen so low? A young soldier just shot an old woman—for no reason. Why? What had she done to deserve that?

From the window of her workshop, Vladka then witnessed something else that had her doubting her eyes. On the street outside flowed a sea of Jews being marched to their death. Thousands were walking past her window. Vladka had seen such roundups before, but nothing as large as this: an endless ocean of human beings, all ages, from tiny children to aging adults, with rags and torn shoes. No one spoke. The only sound was the shuffling of feet.

That week, September 6–12, 1942, was particularly terrible. Special squads of SS and their flunkies had conducted a systematic search of every building and every possible hiding place in the ghetto. Anyone found hiding was rounded up for deportation or else shot on the spot. Dozens of horse-drawn wagons rumbled down the streets and alleys of the ghetto, stopped to pick up corpses, then moved on.

Later, Vladka's comrades in the ŻOB informed her that in those seven days alone, some 60,000 of the ghetto's Jews had been deported and another 6,000 had died from starvation or a German bullet.

The idea of resistance had been whispered about since late 1941 when reports of deaths in concentration camps had first begun to trickle into the ghetto. With the horrific mass slaughter of that week in September, talks of an uprising began in earnest.

Chapter 7

ESCAPE FROM TREBLINKA

One freezing winter morning, there came a knock on Vladka's apartment door. Vladka and her four roommates peered cautiously out and saw an old friend, Elie Lindner, trembling from the cold.

It was November 1942, and the Nazis and their Polish collaborators had dramatically increased their actions in the ghetto. In the previous three months alone, more than 265,000 Jews had been sent by train to the Treblinka death camp. Another 35,000 had been killed inside the ghetto. All Jewish businesses had been closed and the workers deported. Every day, the Nazis rounded up six to seven thousand more Jews and sent them to be murdered.

Elie and his family had been among those deported by train to Treblinka, sixty-five miles from Warsaw. Somehow, he had escaped and made his way back to the ghetto. Vladka and her friends quickly brought him inside and fed him hot soup. Elie told them what had happened to him.

When Elie, his wife, Liebe, and their one-year-old son had arrived at Treblinka, the guards took away all their belongings. Then they marched them, along with the other new arrivals, to a barrack. Guards ordered them to strip and had older prisoners shave off all their body hair. Their next stop was the so-called "showers." By now, Jews knew about the infamous showers in the camps, which released not water but poison gas. Guards pushed Elie's wife and son into one of the so-called showers, along with the other women and children.

When the men's turn came to enter the showers, Elie waited until the guards were looking the other way, then he dove into a pile of discarded clothing and lay perfectly still.

"I waited until there was no more noise," he told Vladka and her roommates, "then I climbed out. Outside the shower bunker, I saw prisoners burying corpses. I ran out and started shoveling, like I was part of their work detail. I managed to stay with them for a few days. Then one night, I hid in another pile of clothes. After dark, I peeked out and saw in the distance the shadow of a freight train. I ran quickly to the train and jumped into one of the cars. The train pulled out, and after several hours I jumped out and walked the rest of the way back to the ghetto. And here I am."

Elie then described more of the horrors he witnessed in

Treblinka. It was not the first time Vladka had heard such stories. Over the last several months, others had escaped and returned with their own gruesome descriptions of what went on there. She tried not to think about such things happening to her mother and siblings. Ever since her family had been deported, Vladka regretted not having gone with them. *The Nazis are going to kill everyone sooner or later anyway*, she told herself. *Why not die with my family?*

One thing and one thing alone stopped her from giving in to such despair: her friends. They were her new family now. No matter how painful and tragic the world around them, they stuck together and never deserted each other in times of need. At least once a day, Vladka's friend Kuba used to tell her, "It's not over yet."

Then one day, Kuba, too, was deported.

Losing Kuba was more than Vladka could bear, and she was forced to admit the situation was hopeless. A handful of Jews against the massive Nazi army? Why go on? She was ready to give up.

But she didn't. Instead, she remembered Kuba's words— "It's not over yet"—and took heart.

Just maybe, she told herself, *there's a way we can fight back.*

Then, one night, Vladka got her chance.

TREBLINKA

To expedite the murder of Europe's Jews, the Nazis built killing centers. Chelmno, in central Poland, opened in December 1941 and was the first camp to murder prisoners with gas. Starting in March 1942, the Germans established three more killing centers—Belzec, Sobibor, and Treblinka—for the purpose of murdering Poland's more than three million Jews.

In July 1942, the Germans completed construction of Treblinka II about fifty miles from the Warsaw ghetto (Treblinka I had been built the year before as a forced-labor camp). The sole purpose of the camp was mass murder.

Between July and September 1942, the Germans deported about 265,000 Jews from the Warsaw ghetto to Treblinka. More Jews arrived at Treblinka from other camps.

Arriving Jews were required to hand over all valuables and clothing. Men were separated from women and children, and all prisoners were forced to run naked along a fenced-in path to the gas chambers, which were deceptively labeled "showers." The chamber doors were sealed shut, and a large diesel engine outside the building pumped carbon monoxide exhaust into the chamber. Everyone inside was killed. The Germans kept a few prisoners alive for the purpose of removing the bodies from the "showers" and burning the bodies in ovens and pits.

By the time Treblinka was dismantled in the fall of 1943, the camp personnel had murdered an estimated 925,000 Jewish men, women, and children.

Chapter 8

A CALL TO ARMS

It had been another grueling twelve-hour shift at the factory. Vladka returned home and found a note under her door.

The note was from Luba Blum, the wife of respected ŻOB leader Abrasha Blum. It said Abrasha wanted to meet Vladka as soon as possible. Could she attend a talk he was scheduled to give that evening?

Vladka didn't hesitate. She immediately walked to the address provided in the note. There, on the street, she met a boy named Luciek Blones.

At thirteen, Luciek was the ŻOB's youngest member, small and thin but dependable and brave. Vladka had heard he was a whiz at finding glass bottles for making Molotov cocktail bombs.

"Follow me," Luciek said. Clearly, he had been waiting for her. "I know the safest way there."

Luciek led Vladka into buildings, down staircases, through cellars and hidden passages, then up staircases, through attics and crawl spaces, out onto rooftops and down fire escapes. When at last they arrived at the fourth-floor headquarters of the ŻOB, they were covered in dust and plaster, but they were on time for Abrasha's talk. The shades had been drawn, and when Abrasha began, the dozen or so attendees went very quiet.

"We must no longer accept deportation," he said. "By now, everyone knows where those freight cars are going. We've all lost family and friends, and sooner or later all of us will likely die as well. But even to die, one must learn how."

Vladka was spellbound listening to him. Abrasha was the very soul of the underground movement in the ghetto. He was tall with a handsome face and piercing eyes, and despite the seriousness of the talk, his soft voice conveyed a sense of assurance and self-confidence.

"True enough, our number is small," Abrasha went on. "Most of our families and friends have been murdered, but we are not alone. I'm here to announce that the other fighting organizations in the ghetto have stepped forward and are prepared to join the ŻOB."

Vladka heard a wave of appreciation sweep through the room. Ever since November 1940, when the Germans sealed the ghetto shut to all outsiders, Jewish organizations inside the ghetto had been at odds with one another. Some groups, such as the Zionists, believed that the way out of the tragedies Jews faced was to create a Jewish state where all Jews could live. Another group, the anti-Zionists, objected, arguing that no single Jewish state could represent the interests of all Jews. There were religious and nonreligious factions as well, each one divided from the others in their tactics, beliefs, and goals for the Jewish people.

Now, Abrasha explained, these diverse groups finally understood that no one could afford to bicker anymore. They had come to a mutually agreeable conclusion: they would reject passivity and compliance and rise up together against the Germans, in the spirit of the biblical warriors David, who fought the giant Goliath, and Joshua, who brought down the walls of Jericho.

Vladka calculated the total number of fighters in these various underground organizations, and her heart beat faster. She knew that when it was first formed in 1940, the ŻOB had only about 200 members. Now, adding up members of the Jewish Military Union and other groups, she estimated the total to be at least 700—more than enough to bring down a few Germans before getting killed themselves.

"From now on," Abrasha told the group, "we work together.

You will receive training for the resistance. Our main job is, one, to get weapons and, two, to contact sympathetic Polish people outside the ghetto who will agree to hide our women and children. Once the uprising begins, mothers and children must be kept away from the fighting."

A discussion broke out about who could best handle which responsibilities.

After the meeting, Abrasha came up to Vladka. "There is something important you could do outside the ghetto," he said. "Are you willing?"

Vladka took a deep breath. "Of course!" she said. "What can I do?"

"Someone will come to your place soon and give you more details."

Vladka clasped Abrasha's hands with tears in her eyes, then she returned home.

That moment was a turning point. Every day since losing her family, Vladka had wanted to do something more than just survive another day. She wanted her life to have meaning. She wanted to fight.

Finally, an opportunity had come that would let her do her part. Finally, she could fight back.

Chapter 9

ESCAPE FROM THE GHETTO

A few nights later, Michal Klepfisz, an important member of the underground, knocked on Vladka's door.

"Get ready," he told her. "You're leaving the ghetto in two days to go live on the other side. We've prepared documents and made other arrangements for you."

Escape from the ghetto—is that possible? Vladka wondered. She knew of many Jews who had attempted to do so. Only a handful ever succeeded. Most had been caught and shot or sent straight to a concentration camp.

Even if she did succeed, what would life be like on the other side of the ghetto wall? That side was no longer the same Warsaw where she'd grown up, where Jews were allowed to live peacefully with non-Jews. Now, any Jew caught outside the ghetto was arrested, deported, and murdered.

Vladka reminded herself that the few Jews who had succeeded in escaping from the ghetto did so because they had money, "Aryan" looks, and spoke flawless Polish. She had all three. Still, even with those advantages, she would also need a job, a place to stay, and friends on the outside.

Michal explained that her first step would be to visit a young man in the ghetto named Ben, who lived with his parents. "Ben is a construction worker," Michal said. "He knows all the foremen working outside the ghetto and will find the right one to help you."

The next evening, Vladka went to go visit Ben. She knew that if a person was careful, it was possible to circulate around the ghetto between 6 and 8 p.m., when the German guards were between shifts. She waited till then, slipped silently out of her apartment, and made her way to Ben's home. He had been sleeping and didn't look his best when Vladka knocked on his door. Still, she liked what she saw and had heard good things about him. When she explained what the underground wanted her to do, Ben agreed to help.

Each morning, Ben explained, he and his work crew followed the same routine. They showed up at the gates of the ghetto, and once police had checked their papers, the crew climbed into horse-drawn wagons and were taken to places around Warsaw where buildings had been demolished. Their job was to collect bricks from the debris and clean them for use by the Germans in new construction. In the evening, after twelve hours or more of hard labor, guards took them back to the ghetto.

"I know most of the officials working outside the ghetto," Ben said. "The foremen, the guards, the police—they all love bribes. I give them some money or a pocket watch or a bottle of vodka, and they look the other way when I need them to."

Ben told Vladka to be at the gates of the ghetto at seven o'clock the next morning and gave her 100 zlotys to bribe the foreman of a particular crew. The foreman, he explained, would then tell the police she was their cook. Then, once they were cleared to exit the ghetto, she was to wait for the right moment, remove her armband with the Jewish star, and disappear into the crowds.

"Good luck," Ben said.

On December 5, 1942, at 7 a.m., Vladka said a tearful goodbye to her roommates. They promised to never forget one another, and she left, arriving a short time later at the ghetto gates. Hidden in her shoes was a top-secret report, written on several sheets of paper, describing the operations of the Treblinka death camp. Her assignment was to deliver the report to underground fighters outside the ghetto.

As Ben had described, the foreman was waiting for her. She slipped him the 100 zlotys, he took her by the arm, and put her in with his crew. Vladka was the only woman in a squad of forty workers, and a curious policeman approached. He poked a finger at the foreman and nodded his head toward Vladka.

"How is it you have a woman worker?" he asked.

"She's the cook in our factory kitchen," the foreman lied.

The policeman walked up and looked closely at Vladka. "I don't like your face," he said, and pointed to a small wooden guardhouse. "Get in there."

Vladka's heart pounded with fear as she walked to the guardhouse, cautiously entered, and peered around. The little wooden office was lit by a bare electric bulb. A small table and chair stood in the center of the room, and on the table were papers and articles of clothing. Clearly, the clothes had been confiscated from other workers who had been put through the inspection she was about to get. It was just as clear what would happen if she didn't cooperate. The walls were splattered with blood.

A guard walked in and sat behind the table. "First and last name," he demanded, and Vladka answered.

"Place of work," he snapped. Vladka told him the name of the workshop where her group was headed that day.

"Take off your clothes," the guard barked.

Vladka had to stop herself from gasping. Apart from being terrified of standing naked in front of this man, the Treblinka report was hidden in her shoes. If the guard found the papers he would kill her and punish everyone in her work detail. Slowly, she took off her coat, then her dress, and handed them to him. He examined the items closely, searching the hems and pockets.

"Shoes," he ordered.

She bent down and, as slowly as she dared, began unlacing her shoes.

"Hurry up!" the guard yelled, holding up a whip.

At that moment, the door flew open.

"Herr Lieutenant," a soldier said. "A Jew has just escaped!"

The soldier and the lieutenant dashed out of the guardhouse. Quickly, Vladka dressed and hurried out. Another guard stopped her.

"Where are you going?" he demanded.

"Back to my work group," she said. "I passed the inspection."

The guard waved her on.

Soon, she was sitting with other workers in the back of a horse-drawn wagon as it rolled through the streets of Warsaw. The wagon came to a crossing and stopped. When none of the guards were looking, Vladka jumped down, tore off her armband with the Jewish star, threw it to the ground, and walked briskly away, blending in with the morning rush of people heading to work.

She was out.

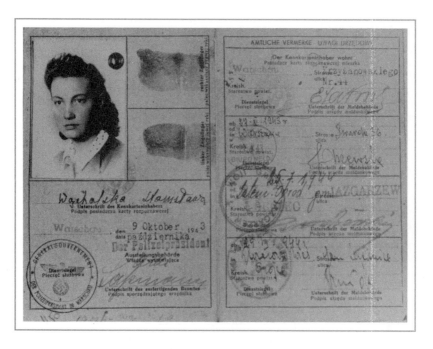

1943—Vladka's false identity card, which allowed her to live and work outside the ghetto wall.

Chapter 10

IN DISGUISE AGAIN

As she walked, Vladka tried her best to look normal and not draw attention to herself. She was back in a world that was both comfortably familiar and uncomfortably alien. She had lived here before—most of her life, in fact. Now, like then, stores were open. Now, like then, women walked by cradling bags of fresh bread and children hurried to school, their backpacks jostling on their shoulders. She had forgotten what Warsaw looked like. Everything had turned strange. Was the ghetto nothing but a dream? Was this real life, or was *that* real life?

Quickly, she snapped out of her daze. She did not want to appear lost or confused to the Polish people around her. The slightest mistake might give her away. She understood that it was the way she carried herself, more than her so-called Aryan features, that would save her or betray her.

She walked as confidently as she could to the address where she was to meet Michal Klepfisz and knocked on the door. Michal peeked out, scanned both sides of the street, then quickly pulled Vladka in before anyone could see them together. She was in a tiny cellar apartment. Michal introduced her to his landlord, a Polish friend from before the war, who had agreed to let Michal stay with him in the small basement living space.

Vladka looked around the tiny space and remembered how beautiful her family's apartment was when she was growing up in Warsaw, not very far from the spot where she stood, and how safe she had felt then. Now, she was a stranger in her own city, hunted like quarry.

To help her begin her new life as a non-Jew, Michal handed her an old passport made out to someone named Wladyslawa Kowalska—"Vladka" for short. And that was how Feige Peltel got the code name Vladka.

If she was going to be effective as an agent for the ŻOB outside the ghetto, she would still need a job, a work permit, and a place to live. She couldn't stay with Michal in the tiny basement apartment. She had to find her own place.

Finding a place to live was almost impossible for a Jew in Nazi-occupied Warsaw. Polish landlords were notorious for their antisemitism, and if they discovered that someone looking to rent a room from them was a Jew in disguise, they called the police. The Germans paid informants a reward of 100 zlotys for every Jew they turned in.

Even if Vladka could convince a landlord to rent her a room, there were blackmailers walking around Warsaw who had a knack for seeing through disguises. When they found Jews trying to pass as non-Jews, the blackmailers demanded a hefty fee to stay quiet. If the Jews had no money, the blackmailer might settle for an overcoat, shoes, or anything else of value. If the Jews had nothing of value to give, the blackmailer handed them over to the Gestapo and claimed the 100-zloty reward.

For days, Vladka moved from one temporary place to another, until finally she met a sympathetic woman named Wanda who had lost her husband in the First World War. Wanda ran a small tailor shop and was in need of an assistant. When Wanda learned Vladka could sew, she gave her a job as a seamstress and a small room over the shop. The situation was a good one. It gave Vladka a place to live and a job, which qualified her for a residence card and a work permit.

As the weeks went by, Wanda's clients grew accustomed to seeing Vladka in the little shop. She made friends, occasionally put in an appearance at the local church like the good Christian she was supposed to be, and little by little she earned the trust of the Christians around her.

Michal watched carefully to be sure Vladka was creating a believable identity. Finally, satisfied that she had sufficiently integrated herself into the non-Jewish community, he invited her to meet Mikolai Berezowski, a senior member of the Jewish fighting organization outside the ghetto. Mikolai was the liaison between the ghetto and the Polish underground.

One night, Vladka, Michal, and Mikolai met in a restaurant run by nuns from a local convent. Mikolai was an older man, tall and elegantly dressed. Vladka liked his silvery hair, upturned mustache, and intelligent eyes. They spoke in low voices to avoid being overheard. Mikolai leaned across the table.

"I've heard good things about you," he said quietly. "Let me tell you what I think you are ready to do. We would like you to find sympathetic Gentiles, family people, and convince them to hide women and children from the ghetto in their homes."

Vladka had been expecting such an assignment, although it would not be easy to do what Mikolai was asking of her. True, some Poles felt compassion for Jews. A few Poles were even working with the Polish underground to prepare their own uprising against the Nazis. Still, there were obstacles to finding homes for Jewish women and children.

For one, Poles were terrified of the Germans, who they knew would shoot anyone found hiding Jews. Few Christian families were willing to take that risk no matter how big the payoff.

For another, not all Jewish parents in the ghetto were prepared to entrust their children to non-Jewish strangers, even if meant saving their children's lives. Some Jewish parents, particularly those who were extremely religious, weren't sure whether it was worse to lose their children to a bullet or conversion to Christianity.

With this new mission, Vladka returned to the ghetto. By now she had become an expert in paying off police and sneaking back and forth over the ghetto wall.

She started with what she hoped would be an easy case: a friend named Manya who had a young son named Artek.

"I will find Artek a good home outside the ghetto," Vladka promised.

Manya refused. "My son and I have endured so much together," she said. "Without me, he would perish."

Vladka did not insist. Who could insist that a mother surrender her own child?

Vladka had better luck with a one-year-old girl, Krysia, whose parents had been murdered by the Nazis. When a Polish family in the suburbs of Warsaw heard that Vladka was offering to pay them 2,500 zlotys each month, they agreed to take Krysia in with them. Vladka followed up for the first few months and was disturbed by what she found. The Polish couple let Krysia wander around unbathed, undernourished, and dressed in rags. The conditions were wretched, but still, living with the Polish couple was safer for Krysia than living in the ghetto.

Over the next several months, Vladka succeeded in placing dozens of Jewish women and children in Polish homes. Her effective handling of these first assignments earned her another meeting with Mikolai in the convent restaurant.

"Now we need you to purchase weapons," Mikolai said, "and deliver them to the ghetto. There can be no uprising without weapons. Be cautious, trust no one, and report to me regularly."

Vladka agreed and headed back to her little room over the tailor shop. The conversation with Mikolai had been polite and subdued, yet the promotion to gunrunner had her excited. She was becoming part of something truly big and important.

The next day, Vladka was in Michal's cellar apartment with others from the ŻOB, when a well-dressed young man arrived with several wooden crates. Michal embraced the young man and introduced him as Aryeh Wilner, head of the ŻOB outside the ghetto wall.

"This is Vladka," Michal said. "She recently escaped from the ghetto."

Aryeh nodded at Vladka, acknowledging the risks she had taken. "May your efforts be blessed with *mazel*," he said, using the Yiddish word for luck.

Michal opened the crates Aryeh had brought and let out a cry of joy. They contained ten revolvers: a priceless treasure and the first delivery of weapons that had been promised by the Polish underground.

Most Poles at that time were very prejudiced toward Jews and did not care to make a place for them in Poland's future. As a consequence, it had taken months of negotiation to achieve a partnership between the ŻOB and the Polish underground officials outside the ghetto.

The celebration was short lived. Only a few days later, Vladka learned that Aryeh had been arrested. Losing him was a severe blow to their preparations for the uprising. But things took a small turn for the better later that week, when

Vladka succeeded in purchasing an old revolver for 2,000 zlotys. The revolver was her first purchase of a weapon for the underground.

In the weeks ahead, she would find and purchase many more—enough to help spark one of the most daring rebellions in history.

1940s—Vladka disguised as a Gentile in Warsaw.

Chapter 11

A MILLION DOLLARS IN A SHOEBOX

Buying weapons was only half of Vladka's assignment. Getting them into the ghetto was the other half. It was nearly impossible for Jews to get back inside the ghetto while carrying a package of any kind. German guards at the ghetto gates were meticulous in their inspections, and the penalty for being found with a weapon was death.

As a result, there was a thriving business going on around the ghetto wall, with Christian smugglers offering to help Jews for the right price. Anyone with a package to smuggle in first had to pay off the leaders of the Polish smugglers. Then there was additional money needed to pay German police to look the other way. Cash was constantly needed to finance the work.

The ŻOB and the Polish underground had supporters as far away as England and America, and sometimes large sums of cash arrived. Vladka was surprised to learn that occasionally the money arrived in shoeboxes that were dropped by parachute into the fields around Warsaw. Once, out of curiosity, she peeked inside a shoebox she was to deliver to the ŻOB and could hardly believe her eyes. The box contained stacks of $100 bills that totaled $50,000. This was in 1942. The equivalent in today's money would be more than $1 million.

One evening, toward the end of that year, Vladka waited in shadows outside the ghetto wall. Hidden in the lining of her jacket were packets of money and reports she was to bring to her friend, Abrasha Blum, inside the ghetto.

An older man carrying a ladder approached her. He was one of the "smugglers" who, for a fee, helped people get in and out of the ghetto. Vladka handed him 75 zlotys, the man positioned his ladder against the ghetto wall, and Vladka quickly climbed. At this spot, the wall was shorter than its usual ten feet and she had no problem jumping down. It took only a few seconds to find herself back inside the ghetto.

Despite the severe shortages of food and medicine in the ghetto, and despite the constant threats of deportation, Vladka felt more at home in the ghetto than she did in the world outside, with all its comforts. In the ghetto she was not obliged to listen to people's spiteful comments about

Jews "getting what they deserved" or praising Hitler for ridding Poland of the "Jewish plague." In the ghetto, she was with her own people.

She continued down the street and ran into someone she recognized, Luciek Blones—the thirteen-year-old boy who was the youngest member of the ŻOB.

Luciek led Vladka to a small apartment where Abrasha greeted her warmly. She handed him the money and reports, and as he read, his face went dark. It was not good news. The Germans planned to liquidate the ghetto by spring of 1943, less than three months from now.

"We have to get the women and children out of here—and quickly," he said.

Abrasha took Vladka into an adjoining room, and there she greeted Luciek's older brother, Yurek, and older sister, Gutta, who gave her a bowl of potato soup and a slice of bread. Around her, trainees made Molotov cocktail bombs by pouring explosives into the glass bottles that Luciek had brought.

Marek Edelman, a commander of the resistance group, handed Vladka a small packet of jewelry. "Get the best price you can for these on the black market," he told her. "Then buy guns, as many as possible."

It was time for Vladka to return to the world outside the

ghetto. The streets were dark when she and Yurek arrived back at the wall. A group of smugglers with a ladder were huddled together against the cold. Yurek approached and asked if this was a good moment for his friend to cross over.

"Wait a bit," one of the smugglers said. "The police have been snooping around."

Yurek and Vladka crossed the street and found a place to wait in an abandoned building. They had a good view of the wall and watched as a woman approached and handed money to one of the smugglers. He positioned his ladder, and she scurried up and dropped out of sight on the other side.

Vladka rose, ready to follow the woman over the wall.

"Wait," Yurek said. "Not yet."

A second woman appeared, handed over money, and started to climb. Before she could reach the top of the ladder, shots rang out. Vladka and Yurek flattened themselves against the wall of their hiding place and waited. The gunfire stopped. Slowly they raised themselves high enough to peer cautiously through a window. The second woman was lying at the base of the ghetto wall in a pool of blood.

If Yurek hadn't stopped me, Vladka realized, *that would be me lying there.*

There was no time for fear or grief. Vladka gave Yurek

a quick hug goodbye, ran to the ladder, handed over the money, climbed swiftly to the top, and jumped. She was back outside the ghetto, among people who would gladly see her dead for a handful of zlotys.

Circa 1942—Smugglers climbing over the Warsaw Ghetto Wall.

JEWISH CHILDREN DURING THE HOLOCAUST

Jewish children were especially vulnerable to Nazi persecution. Most of the 1.5 million Jewish children who died in the Holocaust were murdered simply because they were Jewish. Others died from starvation, disease, or lack of adequate clothing and shelter.

Most children were too young to be used for forced labor, so German authorities selected them first, along with the elderly, the ill, and the disabled, for deportation to killing centers. Other children were led to nearby fields, shot, and buried in mass graves.

Polish educator Janusz Korczak, along with his colleague, Stefania Wilczyńska, operated an orphanage inside the Warsaw ghetto. When the deportations began, Korczak refused to abandon the children under their care. He accompanied them on the transport to Treblinka and went with them to their deaths.

Of the almost one million Jewish children in 1939 Poland, only about 5,000 survived, most of them in hiding.

1940—Children in Janusz Korczak's orphanage in the Warsaw ghetto.

An SS soldier harassing a Jewish child attempting to
bring food into the Warsaw ghetto.

Chapter 12

SAD EYES

Vladka had been living as a Gentile for more than two years, and by now, she was accustomed to traveling by streetcar from one part of Warsaw to another. Thanks to her "Aryan" looks and her forged work papers, she had no problem circulating around the city as though she were just another non-Jewish citizen going from home to work and back.

One morning, she boarded a streetcar, took a seat by a window, and the streetcar moved on to its next scheduled stop. When the streetcar came to a halt, she noticed an SS officer standing on the sidewalk and staring at her. Vladka tried to stay calm.

The officer climbed onto the streetcar and ordered the driver to wait. Passengers followed him with their eyes as he walked to Vladka's seat and demanded to see some identification. She handed him her work permit, which he stuffed into his pants pocket without examining it.

"We'll check this out at the police station," he said. "Come with me."

Vladka followed him off the streetcar and onto the sidewalk. She was confident that the forged papers would hold up under casual inspection, but the prospect of the police examining them more closely felt like someone had hit her in the stomach.

To cover her fear, she laughed and said, "You're going to make me late for work."

"Never mind that," the officer said. "You look Jewish. You have sad eyes."

Vladka laughed some more. "How can you say that?" she said. "I come from a good Polish family. We've lived here for generations."

The SS officer hesitated and looked at her again. Passengers watched the exchange from the streetcar windows, and pedestrians slowed down to hear what the officer was saying. The interrogation had begun to draw a crowd.

"Maybe I made a mistake," the officer said, and he handed Vladka back her papers.

Vladka jumped back on the streetcar just as it was pulling away. After that, she was careful to never let her sad eyes give her away.

A few weeks later, she was again put to the test.

The ŻOB sent Vladka by train to a town outside Warsaw to

pick up important documents. The train ride out of Warsaw went smoothly, as did the collection of the documents.

For the return to Warsaw, she showed up early at the train station. She had taped the documents to her back under her blouse, and, as a cover story to explain what she had been doing in the town, she carried three little chicks in a cardboard box. If the police stopped her, she would explain that she was bringing the chicks as a gift from her grandmother to her parents in Warsaw.

Anyone looking to purchase a train ticket in Nazi-occupied Poland had to show a travel card explaining the purpose of their trip. When she was carrying out a mission, Vladka solved that problem by bribing other passengers to buy her a ticket. Times were hard, and people were happy to take her money.

This time, while looking for someone to bribe, she went into the station café and bought a cup of coffee. She noticed an SS officer circulating around the café, checking people's travel documents. *If he finds out I don't have a travel card*, she thought, *that will be the end of me.*

The officer stopped in front of Vladka's table. To cover any hint of "sad eyes," she began flirting with him, batting her eyelids and then turning to the side, pretending to not see him looking at her. The officer pulled out a chair.

"Do you mind if I sit with you?" he asked.

"Why should I mind such a handsome young officer sitting with me?" she told him with a smile. The chicks started up.

"Cheep! Cheep! Cheep!"

The officer reached down and opened the box. "Where are you going with those?" he asked.

"A gift, from my grandmother to my parents in Warsaw."

The officer looked at her and smiled. "Did you buy your ticket yet?"

"No," she said innocently.

"If I buy you your ticket, will you have a date with me in Warsaw?"

"Of course!" Vladka said with a big smile. She gave him a false address, the officer bought her a ticket, escorted her to the train, and they waved goodbye.

Vladka noticed that two elderly Polish women had been watching the exchange. After the officer left, one poked the other with her elbow and said, "If you looked as good as her, you wouldn't have to buy a ticket, either."

If the circumstances had been different, Vladka might have laughed.

Chapter 13

RISE UP!

Rat-a-tat-tat! Rat-a-tat-tat!

From the window of her apartment near the ghetto wall, Vladka heard machine guns. She peeked outside and saw police setting up wooden barricades to stop all traffic going into or coming out of the ghetto.

By now, residents of Warsaw had grown accustomed to hearing short bursts of machine guns. More often than not, the shots came from Nazi soldiers looking to scare people.

This gunfire, though, wasn't stopping. It went on and on, as if encountering resistance. What was happening?

The explanation came a short time later. ŻOB leader Michal Klepfisz sneaked out of the ghetto and showed up at Vladka's apartment with an incredible report: German soldiers had been conducting another roundup in the ghetto, he said, and were marching their prisoners to the train station for deportation to concentration camps. What happened next was as much of a shock to the people in the ghetto as it was to the Germans. Jewish fighters hiding in nearby buildings jumped out and opened fire. They killed several German soldiers and forced the other soldiers to flee. The Jewish prisoners broke free from their captors, ran down alleyways, and escaped into buildings.

This was the first time Jews in the ghetto had fought back against the Nazis, and it had an immediate effect on the rest of the ghetto population. Jews who had previously done nothing to support the ŻOB, thinking resistance was impossible, now stepped forward and offered jewelry to help purchase weapons. Others volunteered to build bunkers and barricades. Still others began cooking meals for the fighters. Some helped prepare homemade bombs. Others took turns standing lookout on rooftops and from behind windows. That one act of resistance finally convinced the ghetto's terrified population that maybe Jews could, after all, control a bit of their own destiny.

Vladka and the other members of her group knew the Germans would return to avenge the attack and would not stop until Warsaw was *Judenrein*, a German phrase coined by the Nazis that meant "cleared of all Jews."

By now there were about five hundred ŻOB fighters in the Warsaw ghetto. Even though the fighters were divided among more than two dozen groups, the demonstration of defiance was bringing them together. That one successful rebellion united the ghetto fighters into a single, cooperative movement. They were now, more than at any time since the construction of the ghetto, ready to stage a true uprising.

But they were still in desperate need of weapons.

Chapter 14

DYNAMITE

Vladka knew that the ŻOB had pleaded with the Polish underground to share their weapons, and that the Polish leadership had refused. All weapons were being stockpiled for the bigger uprising, the leaders explained, which was expected to begin soon. This bigger uprising was the one that would unite all of Poland against the Nazis, and no weapons could be spared for Jews in the ghetto.

The British government had also declined to supply weapons, claiming that England was committed to winning the war against Germany and that none of their arms could be detoured for any other purpose.

Vladka's unsuccessful attempts to purchase weapons underscored just how hopeless the ŻOB's position was: a few hundred inexperienced volunteers armed with a box of pistols, daring to rise up against thousands of seasoned Nazi soldiers armed with tanks, fighter planes, machine guns, and unlimited supplies of bullets and bombs.

One night in the spring of 1943, Vladka made her final attempt to secure weapons. It was also her most dangerous. She had failed to find any guns for sale, but she found something just as good if not better: In a cloth bag slung over her shoulder were ten pounds of dynamite.

The sky was still dark in the hours just before sunrise as Vladka ran silently to an old wooden ladder propped against the ghetto wall. She handed the chief smuggler a fistful of zlotys, climbed the rungs of the ladder, and pulled herself up onto the top edge of the wall. She checked her bag. The dynamite was safe and well hidden. She had wrapped the dozen or so explosive sticks in grease paper. To a casual observer, it would look like she was carrying slabs of meat or large sticks of butter.

In the darkness, she squinted at the ghetto side of the wall. Where were her comrades, Yurek and Yanek? They were supposed to help her climb down. The street was empty. Just then, shots rang out. Vladka looked back over her shoulder and shuddered. The ladder was gone! The smugglers had heard the gunfire, snatched their ladder, and run away, leaving her stranded atop the high wall, holding the slippery package of dynamite. She could try to jump, but she didn't know much about dynamite and was terrified it would explode when she hit the ground. Her heart was ready to burst from her chest. The gunfire started up again, this time closer and louder.

This is it, she told herself. *I'm dead.*

Suddenly, she heard familiar voices.

"Quick, Vladka! Quick!"

It was Yurek and Yanek. They had been hiding and were now standing at the bottom of the wall. One climbed onto the shoulders of the other, making a human ladder, and quickly Vladka climbed down into the ghetto. In the distance, she saw German guards running toward them and firing their pistols.

The three friends sprinted to an empty building across from the wall, burst through the door, and scrambled up the wooden stairs to a dusty attic. In one corner, they saw ripped pillows and a huge pile of feathers. They flew across the attic, dove into the pile of feathers, and lay perfectly still. They heard boots stomping up the stairs, soldiers tossing furniture, searching everywhere. A few minutes later, the soldiers left.

Vladka and her two friends slowly emerged from the mountain of feathers, crawled cautiously out of the building, ran across courtyards, up staircases, through abandoned apartments, down flights of stairs, and out onto busy streets. The sun was just rising, and they blended with ghetto residents on their way to work.

The three young fighters finally made their way to ŻOB headquarters, where Vladka delivered the dynamite to a grateful Abrasha Blum. Then she sprawled out on the floor, exhausted. Around her, young men and women were grabbing stacks of flyers and heading out the door. She picked up one of the flyers and read:

The Jewish Fighting Organization calls on all ghetto residents to refuse German orders. Jews! Do not let yourself be taken! The so-called labor camps are all death camps! Resist!

—The ŻOB

The message was an impassioned plea for the entire Warsaw ghetto to join the uprising. With her remaining bit of strength, Vladka took a pile of flyers and headed out the door.

The ghetto was alive with activity. Jewish men, women, and children were hard at work, building wooden barricades and positioning them at intersections to slow down the passage of German armored cars and trucks. Other residents were hammering wooden boards across windows. A group of older Jews huddled around a flyer someone had posted on a wall and one person read it out loud for others to hear. From time to time, they looked warily to their left and right, to be sure no police were watching, then returned to reading the flyer.

One elderly man walked quietly up to Vladka and asked, "Do you know where we can get guns?"

Vladka was exhausted, but she felt intense pride over what the ŻOB had managed to do. Their call to action had united the entire ghetto. For herself, there was no time to rest. No time to think too much. Sooner or later, she told herself, she too would be killed. Better to focus on the task at hand, whatever it might be.

Circa 1941—Climbing over the ghetto wall. Going in and out became more difficult after November 15, 1940, when the ghetto was "sealed" and only people with special permits were allowed to leave or return.

Chapter 15

THE WARSAW GHETTO UPRISING

When at last the uprising began on the morning of April 19, 1943, Vladka was furious at herself. After months of preparation, she was on the wrong side of the wall.

In a final attempt to buy weapons, she and her comrades had climbed over the wall and searched for days outside the ghetto, but without success. There were no weapons for sale at any price. When they were ready to climb back into the ghetto, they approached the wall, expecting to find smugglers and a ladder. Instead, they found dozens of SS troops in full battle gear surrounding the wall and blocking the entrances.

For years, Vladka and her fellow ŻOB fighters had prepared to be part of the uprising inside the ghetto. To now find herself on the wrong side of the ghetto wall was beyond infuriating.

From where she stood on the street, Vladka could see German tanks rolling through the ghetto gates, shooting at anything that moved. Vehicles with mounted machine guns crisscrossed the ghetto, firing at random into the buildings. Hundreds of soldiers advanced in straight lines, their flamethrowers sending fierce arcs of fire into apartment windows.

Vladka heard a loud droning sound. She looked up and saw German fighter planes flying low and dropping incendiary bombs into the ghetto. The ground shook with the explosions, and a thick cloud of black smoke rose up from the rubble and blocked out the sun.

Vladka listened to the gunfire and noted that the *rat-a-tat-tat* coming from German machine guns was punctuated by the crack of single bullets, the crash of glass, and the whoosh of flames. *It's finally happening*, she thought. *Jews equipped with nothing but a handful of small firearms and homemade gasoline bombs are actually fighting back against the German army.*

Vladka and her fellow underground members outside the ghetto quickly gathered in another member's apartment. From the window, they watched with a combination of pride and frustration. They were supposed to be in there, fighting side by side with their friends.

They saw a stream of ambulances emerge from the ghetto, transporting wounded German soldiers to field hospitals. A Polish spectator on the street said what many of the other Polish citizens were thinking:

"Can you believe that? The Jews have done some damage!"

No one had expected the poorly equipped, inexperienced Jewish underground to cause havoc to the mighty German army.

Inside the ghetto, there was one phone located in a hairbrush factory that allowed the ŻOB to communicate with their counterparts outside the wall. Around midnight, Mikolai, the senior underground representative to whom Vladka reported, received a call from Abrasha Blum from inside the ghetto. Mikolai gathered Vladka and the other underground fighters together and told them what he had learned.

"Abrasha reports that active resistance inside the ghetto has begun," Mikolai said. "All the fighting groups are cooperating and it's all very well organized. Only a few casualties among our fighters. Far more among the Germans."

A second call came on the night of the third day of fighting. "A difficult day," Abrasha told Mikolai. "Short on ammunition. We need more arms!" Then he quickly hung up.

Vladka was desperate to know more about what was happening inside the ghetto. She remembered that a Christian family named Dubiel who lived nearby had adopted Jewish children—and they had a phone. She hurried to their apartment. When she arrived, she dialed the ghetto factory and was given tragic news. The Germans were winning the battle. Several people in the underground had taken their own lives rather than let themselves be captured. Among those killed by German soldiers was her dear friend Michal Klepfisz. Then the phone went dead.

On the fifth day of the uprising, Vladka attended an emergency meeting of the ŻOB. Even though she and her comrades were stranded outside the ghetto, they agreed there were still things they could do to help. For one, they could spread news of the uprising. The world needed to know what was going on.

They settled on a plan to print posters that read THE GHETTO IS FIGHTING BACK, THE STRUGGLE FOR YOUR FREEDOM AND OURS CONTINUES and glue them to buildings throughout Warsaw. At least the Polish people would learn what was happening. Jews were not loved by most Poles, but the Nazis were their common enemy, and ŻOB fighters dreamed of the day when Jewish and non-Jewish Poles would fight side by side against the Nazi murderers.

Vladka brought money and the text for the poster to a sympathetic printer not far from the ghetto wall. It was Palm Sunday, a week before Easter, and as she returned from the printshop Vladka saw parents coming out of church services with their children. The priest was standing at the church door, shaking people's hands and thanking them for coming.

On the public square, only a hundred feet or so from the ghetto wall, was a merry-go-round. Parents lifted their children up onto wooden horses and smiled, watching them ride round and round. The parents knew the ghetto was burning. They could see the flames leaping into the sky. They could hear the gunfire and smell the smoke. They could even feel the intense heat, but they were busy enjoying a spring day with their children and had no time or pity for dying Jews.

Vladka heard one parent say to another, calmly pointing to the flames raging on the other side of the wall, "Look at that. The Jews are frying today."

That night, Vladka looked out from the window of the Dubiels' apartment and gazed at the terrifying spectacle of flames and smoke rising up from inside the ghetto, turning the sky over Warsaw dark crimson. Looking down onto the streets of the ghetto, she saw burned corpses. She watched a soldier walk by the bodies with a machine gun. Whenever he saw a body move, he sprayed it with bullets.

By day six of the uprising, Vladka's life had become one long frustration. There were no weapons to be bought, and even if there were, there was no way to smuggle them into the ghetto. Her days were reduced to waiting and watching German planes fly over the ghetto and rain down bombs that reduced any remaining buildings to rubble.

One morning, from the window of the Dubiels' apartment, she looked into the ghetto and saw a woman on the second-floor balcony of a burning house. The woman held a child in one arm, and with the other she dropped a feather mattress onto the pavement.

Is she planning to jump with the child, Vladka wondered, *and hopes the mattress will break their fall?*

The woman began climbing over the balcony railing. Vladka heard a burst of machine gun fire and saw the woman go limp. The child dropped from her arms. In minutes, flames spread, consuming what remained of the second floor.

On the eleventh day of the uprising, two of the fighters, Zygmunt and Kazik, escaped the ghetto through sewer pipes. They emerged from the sewer and looked back to find the sky over the ghetto still glowing from fires that had destroyed everything and everyone.

They had been given Vladka's address. The two young men quickly arrived at her small apartment and described for her how the Germans were murdering the Jews of the ghetto street by street. They and five other fighters had been hiding in the hairbrush factory. Under the brick pavement outside the shop, they had buried their one land mine. A column of German soldiers marched toward the shop, coming closer and closer, until they stood over the land mine in front of the shop. Kazik connected the two wires of the detonator. A huge blast shook the street. Plaster and glass rained down. When the dust settled, Kazik saw dozens of dead Germans, their clothes, helmets, and rifles strewn everywhere.

"The German army may have destroyed most of Europe," Kazik told Vladka, "but they didn't expect such resistance from a bunch of Jews. We've been fighting them with whatever guns and grenades we have, and for a while we were holding them off. But the Germans stopped trying to control the ghetto from the streets and instead came at us from the sky, using dive-bombers and incendiary bombs. Then they came back into the ghetto and finished the job with flamethrowers.

"We ran out of weapons and hid underground," Kazik went on. "The Germans found the air shaft leading to our bunker and used it to toss hand grenades down at us. With us was a nineteen-year-old, David Hochberg, who bravely used his own body to block the air shaft. The Germans shot him, but by the time they could dig his body out of the opening, the other Jews had escaped through the sewers. That's how we got here, thanks to him."

Eventually, seventy men and women escaped from the ghetto through sewer pipes and took shelter in the woods outside Warsaw. There, they divided themselves up into smaller units and joined Polish partisan groups.

A week later, Vladka paid another visit to the Dubiel family. From their window, she peered over the ghetto wall just in time to see German soldiers uncover the entrance to a second bunker and force Jews who had been hiding there out onto the street. The soldiers lined their prisoners up against a brick wall. An Orthodox Jewish man with a long beard stood at the wall, a little boy at his side, mostly likely his son. A policeman ordered the boy to stand at a spot some distance from the old man. The father refused to let the boy go. He held him tightly with one hand, and with the other he reached up toward heaven. The policeman pulled out his gun and fired. The image of the father and son falling to the ground seared itself into Vladka's mind, where it would remain for the rest of her life.

Vladka was one of a small group of Jews who had done everything in their power to fight the Nazis. It was a battle they knew could not be won, and now, watching atrocity after atrocity, she felt isolated, useless, and lonely. Her friends and family had been murdered, the world she once knew was gone forever, and nothing she could do would ever bring it back.

Chapter 16

THE END

The end of the uprising came on May 8, 1943. By then, the Germans had so completely destroyed the ghetto that hardly any buildings were still standing. The destruction of the ghetto had been carried out under the direction of SS General Jürgen Stroop. In his official report about the massacre to his Nazi superiors, Stroop proudly wrote, "The Jewish quarter of Warsaw is no more!"

In the days that followed the end of the ghetto, Vladka walked the streets of Warsaw, feeling bitter and furious. *Why am I still alive?* she thought. *I should have died with my friends.*

As she passed by Polish people, she heard them say things like, "Well, at least the Germans took care of the Jewish problem for us," and she felt even angrier that she hadn't died fighting inside the ghetto. Her friends had died from bullets and smoke and flames and poison gas, and the guilt she felt over still being alive was unbearable.

Sometime later, Vladka received a copy of a letter composed in the underground bunker by ŻOB Commander Mordecai Anielewicz, shortly before he died. He'd written the letter to Antek (Itzak) Zuckerman, a friend and ŻOB leader.

Dear Itzak,

Let us leave out personal matters at this time. What I wish most to share is what my comrades and I feel. Something had happened beyond our wildest dreams. Twice the Germans were forced to flee the ghetto. The dream of my life has become a reality. I have lived to see the Jewish defense in the ghetto in all its greatness and splendor.

Mordecai

Vladka read the letter a second time, then a third. Mordecai knew he was going to die when he wrote it, and yet he described the "greatness" and "splendor" of the uprising as "the dream of my life." What an extraordinary thing, and how grateful she felt to be reminded that the "greatness" of the Jews was not a question of numbers, and that the "splendor" of their actions placed them at the opposite extreme from the ugliness of the Germans. Above all, his words reminded her of the bravery with which her friends had met their death.

His words also gave Vladka a reason to keep going. Someday, she decided, she would tell the story of those who hadn't survived.

1943—One of the most famous pictures of World War II, showing Jews captured by Germans during the suppression of the Warsaw Ghetto Uprising.

Chapter 17

ARRESTED

The Nazis leveled the ghetto with flames on the ground and bombs from the sky. They destroyed in one month what had taken the Jews of Poland a thousand years to build, and still the Nazis were not done. Now they turned their attention outside the ghetto, where they murdered any remaining Jews in hiding, bulldozed Warsaw's synagogues, and torched Jewish libraries. Nothing would stop them until they had erased the very memory of Jewish culture.

Vladka and her comrades in the ŻOB had lost the ghetto, but one task remained: to bring help to the few thousand Jews who were still alive outside the ghetto.

As always, her great inspiration was Abrasha Blum, whom she saw as the heart and soul of the ŻOB. Abrasha was among the few fighters who had survived the burning of the ghetto. He had been in the group that had escaped through the sewer and made their way to the woods surrounding Warsaw. Without shelter, his health had quickly deteriorated and at the request of his wife, Vladka agreed to hide him in her apartment until he recovered.

It wasn't long after he arrived that the floorboards of her small apartment shook from boots marching up the stairs. Then banging rattled her door.

"Open up!"

"This is it," she whispered to Abrasha. "They've come for us. Hide."

Abrasha slid into a closet and shut the door.

Vladka felt proud that such an important person would be hiding in her place, but she'd known from the outset it was not safe. Landlords had strict rules about visitors, and any new face showing up at Vladka's apartment could bring the police. But Abrasha was a commander of the ghetto fighters, critical to the uprising, and there had been no choice but to take him in.

"Open the door immediately!"

Vladka unlatched the apartment door, and in strode a Gestapo officer and a policeman.

"Where's the Jew?" the Gestapo officer demanded.

"There's nobody here but me," she lied. "My fiancé is usually here, but he's away on business just now."

"We'll see."

It took only a minute for them to find Abrasha hiding in the closet.

"The van will be here soon to take you both to the police station," the Gestapo officer said. The two men helped themselves to everything of value they could find, then left and locked the apartment from the outside.

"Abrasha, I have anti-Nazi pamphlets hidden in my wall," Vladka said. "If the police come back and find them, they'll know we work for the underground. They'll torture us to find out where our comrades are hiding."

They dug the pamphlets out from the wall, burned them in the kitchen sink, then took the ashes and flushed them down the toilet.

"There's only one way we can escape," Abrasha said. "Out the window." He took the sheets off Vladka's bed, knotted them together, then tied one end to the apartment's heavy radiator.

"You should go first," Abrasha said. "You're younger."

"But you have a wife and children," Vladka replied. "Once you're down on the street, I'll follow you."

Abrasha tied the other end of the sheets around his waist and lowered himself out the window. A minute later, the sheets ripped apart and the tall fighter fell to the pavement with a loud crash. Residents in the building heard the noise, ran to their balconies, and saw Abrasha sprawled on the pavement.

"Police! Police!" they yelled, furious that someone in their building had dared to hide a Jew, and now the Germans might punish all of them.

Within minutes, the same Gestapo officer and policeman were banging on Vladka's door. She opened the door and found them holding up Abrasha. His face was bloody and his legs were broken. They drove Vladka and Abrasha to a nearby police station and threw Abrasha into one cell and Vladka into another with a group of women.

"What did they get you for?" one of the women asked.

"Please," Vladka said, "I'm so tired." She put her head on the woman's arm and fell asleep.

In the morning, Vladka was jarred awake by the clang of her cell door opening. The policeman who had arrested her walked in. "We're taking your friend to Gestapo headquarters," he said. "Then we're coming back for you."

Vladka knew that once they were in Gestapo headquarters, there was no hope of ever leaving alive. Then it occurred to her that this police officer did not know she was Jewish. Maybe he even believed the story about her fiancé being out of town and leaving her with a Jew. She walked up to him, reached into her pocket, and handed him whatever money she had.

"Please," she said with her best smile, "take this money for your troubles. I'm being accused of hiding a Jew, but it's a mistake. My fiancé brought this man. I had no idea he was a Jew."

The police officer looked at the wad of zlotys. "Are you sure you didn't know he was a Jew?" he asked.

"I swear I had no idea," she said. "My fiancé just left him there and didn't tell me a thing."

The officer took the money, stuffed it in his pocket, and nodded toward the prison door. Vladka quickly left and made her way back to the apartment.

Vladka would have done anything to help Abrasha, but there was nothing she could do now. She never saw the ŻOB leader again.

Chapter 18

SOMEONE WHO CARES

Soon, Vladka received a troubling order from Mikolai and other ŻOB leaders. The letter thanked her for completing hundreds of successful missions for the underground but said she must now stop what she was doing and leave Warsaw. For one, her old identity papers were no longer valid, and it would take time to get her new ones. For another, she may have attracted too much attention, and it was impossible to know who might betray her.

At least for a while, for her own safety she needed to slow her pace.

Vladka saw the wisdom in their decision and reluctantly agreed. She thought carefully about where to go. Among the handful of sympathetic Christian families with room for a guest, one couple came to mind. They were simple people who operated a farm in a nearby village surrounded by forests. She contacted the couple, and they agreed to let her hide in their home.

At their house, Vladka slept uninterrupted for the first time in weeks. She took leisure walks under the canopies of four-hundred-year-old oak trees, gathered mushrooms and vegetables that grew wild in the forest, made delicious soups that she shared with her hosts, and watched deer, foxes, and rabbits roam nearby fields. At least with trees and animals, she did not have to pretend she was a Gentile.

The combination of uninterrupted sleep, fresh air, and a healthy diet worked wonders. Vladka may have been in better shape than she had known in years, but she could not stand the inaction. In messages back to the underground in Warsaw, she pleaded to be rescued from her isolation. Could she not return and do something meaningful?

Vladka's main contact now was Ben Meed, the young man who had helped her escape the ghetto the very first time. From Ben, she learned the tragic news that the seventy ŻOB fighters who had escaped through the ghetto's sewers were all dead. At first, the fighters tried hiding in forests outside Warsaw, but German bombs had destroyed the older, thicker trees that would have provided effective cover. What remained of the forest were saplings too thin to hide anything. Polish peasants had easily spotted the fighters, informed the authorities, collected their 100-zloty-per-Jew reward, and watched as the Germans shot all seventy prisoners.

Ben often visited Vladka in the countryside. The time they spent together led to mutual affection, and affection led to love. Vladka's hosts on the farm knew love when they saw it, and they invited Ben to move in.

With her family murdered and her comrades deported or worse, for too long Vladka had been alone. Of course, the underground fighters all cared about one another, but they were always aware that their next assignment could be their last. Their friendships were tainted by knowing one of them could be killed any time. Why invest in a relationship that was certain to end in tragedy? With Ben, Vlakda discovered what it meant to have someone who cared deeply if she lived or died.

Vladka found Ben to be intelligent, a wonderful conversationalist, fun, and full of creative ideas. He taught her how to ride a bicycle. He built a hiding place for her behind a full-length mirror. To protect her secret documents, he showed her how to install a false bottom in a desk drawer. And Ben admired Vladka's keen intellect, curiosity, and complete dedication to the cause. They foraged for mushrooms together, cooked meals together, washed clothes together, and shared professional secrets.

One of Vladka's happiest moments during these dark times was the day Ben introduced her to his parents, Israel Yacob and Rivka, and his younger sister, Genia. Ben had managed to sneak his family out of the ghetto and had found a place for them to live in hiding. It was one-half of a small wooden shed on the grounds of a Russian Orthodox cemetery, where Ben worked digging graves and building coffins for the caretaker. One half of the shed was where the caretaker kept his goats, the other half, separated by a wall Ben had built, was for Ben's family.

Ben and Vladka arrived on Friday evening, the start of the Jewish Sabbath. While Ben's mother and sister prepared a modest meal from their few supplies, Ben's father recited prayers, his head covered in the traditional *tallis*, or prayer shawl. The scene reminded Vladka of her own home on the Sabbath, before the ghetto, before the deportations. Though her own family was gone, in the company of Ben's family she felt again a sense of belonging and felt inspired seeing how they had not abandoned their Jewish traditions.

Ben and Vladka may have had a relationship made in heaven, but Ben's parents did not immediately approve. They frowned on their son spending so much time with a girl who was not his wife. If Ben and Vladka were serious about each other, his parents said, they wanted the relationship to be legitimate. One day, Ben's mother showed up and handed Vladka a gold ring.

"This is for you," she said. "Now it's official. Congratulations. You're engaged."

1943—Vladka in the countryside outside Warsaw.

Chapter 19

RISE UP, POLAND!

Vladka and Ben kept their engagement a secret. But there was a different celebration, one not as satisfying, that they were obliged to have. In Poland, Christian parents often named their children after Christian saints. The families would celebrate the birthday of the chosen patron saint with songs and a feast. The name "Vladka" was derived from the name Stanislava, a Christian saint from the eleventh century. To keep up appearances, Vladka and Ben announced they would be celebrating the birth of Saint Stanislava, and their neighbors were invited to attend.

One evening, after the party, Vladka shared with Ben how hard it was for her to continue hiding her true identity. "I don't like having to pretend I'm Christian," she said. "I'm proud of being a Jew. This charade makes me feel invisible and irrelevant."

She thought back on the hundreds of assignments she'd carried out, and then she remembered there was no one left from her former life to share them with. "When I go out on a mission," she said, "sometimes I wonder whether it would matter to anyone if I don't return."

"It would matter to me," Ben said. "I'd miss you terribly if you weren't here. It won't go on like this forever, Vladka, I promise you. Things will change."

Vladka appreciated Ben's reassurances, but they weren't enough. The only words that would make her feel better now were "The war is over" and "The Nazis lost." And who knew when that would happen?

In the summer of 1944, news that the Germans were losing the war with Russia spread through Warsaw. People hardly dared to believe what they were hearing, yet on the roads heading east, Vladka and Ben saw the evidence: wounded, demoralized Nazi soldiers making their way back from Russia to Germany in broken army trucks and horse-drawn wagons. It was amazing. The Russians had defeated the undefeatable Nazi army. The sounds of Russian gunfire and exploding bombs echoed faintly in the distance, but each day the sounds came closer and grew louder.

More good news came by way of reports heard on contraband radios. The Allied forces had landed at Normandy Beach on the coast of France. Energized by a certainty that the tide of the war had turned and that Russian forces would soon arrive, at 5 p.m. on August 1, 1944, a cry went out from rooftops across Warsaw, "Attack the Germans!" Sirens wailed and gunfire erupted on every street corner. The people of Poland were fighting back against their Nazi oppressors.

The surge didn't last.

Days turned into weeks, weeks into months, and still the Russian army failed to appear. What had happened? No one knew, but the delay was fatal. The Polish insurgents were poorly organized and had few weapons, and day by day, the Nazis regained control of Warsaw. The Polish general uprising ended on October 2, 1944, with the surrender of the surviving Polish rebels to German forces.

The uprising had infuriated German leaders. How dare the Poles question Nazi authority? In retaliation, the German army set out to destroy Warsaw. Planes bombarded the city day and night. German soldiers conducted house-to-house searches, killing everyone they found—Jews, non-Jews, men, women, and children—and setting fire to every building in the city. The bombing of Warsaw by Nazi planes swelled, grew louder, darker, until it became an inferno that destroyed everything and everyone in its path. The city was covered by a vast cloud of black smoke. At night the sky burned bright red. The air was unbreathable, a mix of dust, smoke, and the smell of burning human flesh.

When she returned to the city and saw the damage, Vladka found herself reliving the horrors of the destruction of the Warsaw ghetto.

She and Ben had returned to visit Ben's parents and found them preparing to leave, to go wherever fate would take them, rather than waiting to be killed by Nazis or Polish antisemites. Ben's mother and father had each prepared a small bundle of food. Because Ben's mother suffered from severe ailments and could not walk, Ben's father would carry her on his back. The family embraced and said tearful goodbyes, not knowing if they would see each other again.

Throughout the cold, snowy winter of 1944, Vladka and Ben wandered the countryside, pretending to be Gentiles, changing homes frequently to avoid arrest. As a further measure for flushing out Jews in hiding, every few weeks the authorities issued new identity papers. Jews with counterfeit papers could no longer expect to remain undetected. Vladka and Ben had a Gentile friend, Krysha, who worked as a cook in the home of a large Polish family. "If you get the new papers," Krysha told them, "you can stay with me."

Had Vladka and Ben not found a place to live outside the city, had they not succeeded in securing false identity papers and work permits, had Krysha not offered to hide them in her home, if a thousand things had happened differently, they would have been killed along with so many of their family and friends.

Life was no longer a blessing. It had atrophied to mere survival, shriveled down to whatever remained when everything else had been cruelly, persistently, horribly ripped away.

1944—The doomed Warsaw general uprising.

THE POLISH GENERAL UPRISING

The Polish general uprising was a major World War II operation by the Polish Home Army, working to liberate Warsaw from German occupation. It occurred in the summer of 1944 and was timed to coincide with the retreat of the German forces from Poland ahead of the Soviet advance. The Polish uprising was fought for sixty-three days with little outside support.

While approaching the eastern suburbs of the city, leaders of the Soviet Army decided to halt their advance. The delay lasted for months and enabled the Germans to regroup, defeat the Polish resistance, and destroy Warsaw in retaliation for the uprising. Despite its failure, the Polish general uprising is considered the single largest military effort taken by any European resistance movement against the Nazis during World War II.

Chapter 20

WASTELAND

Vladka and Ben were now hiding in the home where their friend Krysha worked, in a village outside Warsaw. Following Krysha's advice, they carefully rehearsed the story they would tell the man in charge of handing out new papers. When their appointment came, their presentation was convincing.

"We're from Warsaw," they said, "but as you know, so many homes were destroyed in the bombing, including ours, and we lost all our papers and possessions in the fire. Our friend Krysha has known us a long time. She's offering us a job and a place to stay, provided you kindly issue us new identity papers."

The officer was convinced by their story and gave them the papers.

As they were leaving his office, Vladka recognized a man coming in: a Jew from Warsaw. Tragically, he had not prepared his story as well, and after hearing him out, the same officer who had just issued Vladka and Ben their new papers drew his gun and shot the man on the spot. Vladka and Ben had to stifle a gasp as they quickly left the office in horror.

Vladka found work as a seamstress in the home of a wealthy family, Ben was hired as a handyman, and for the next several weeks they remained disguised as Christians and attended church services on Sundays. In December, they joined their neighbors in decorating the village Christmas tree, and on Christmas Day, they drank eggnog and sang holiday songs with the other villagers in the town square. They hated every minute of the charade, wishing they could live as their true selves again.

Finally, on January 16, 1945, the Russians advanced to within a few miles of Warsaw. Artillery shells exploded around Vladka and Ben's village, and the earth shook from the impact. In the morning, as the sun rose, Vladka looked out from the window of their small room and saw an amazing sight. Russian tanks were rolling down the streets of their village. In the distance, they saw German soldiers retreating.

"Vladka, it's over," Ben said.

They gathered with others from the village to hear a Russian officer standing on a tank announce in broken Polish, "You are free! Take what you want from the rich!"

The impoverished villagers, who saw little distinction between Nazi oppressors and Polish oppressors, gladly obliged and ransacked the homes of the wealthier people. Some villagers ran off with horses, others wheeled away furniture and clothing, and everybody helped themselves to stocks of food. At first, Ben and Vladka refused to take part in the looting, but that made the Russian officer suspicious.

"Why aren't you two taking anything?" he demanded. "Are you Jews?"

Vladka and Ben grabbed two blankets and two bicycles and immediately set out for Warsaw. Now that they could finally return home, the first thing they had urgently wished to do was visit the ghetto, the place where their friends had fought so valiantly. They knew what they would find there but nonetheless felt compelled to go.

There was no ghetto anymore. What remained was a wasteland of ruins, endless piles of crumbled walls, hills of stones and bricks as far as the eye could see. They climbed through the ruins of what had once been the Jewish cemetery and found thousands of gravestones all upended. Next to the dug-up graves were skulls with teeth missing. Grave robbers had ripped out the gold crowns. Vladka looked for her father's grave, but it was impossible to tell one pile of rocks from another.

Soon after, they left the ghetto to visit the once beautiful city of Warsaw. As inside the ghetto, nothing of the city remained. After sixty-three days and nights of brutal barrages by Nazi artillery and airpower, one of the world's great cities had been reduced to rubble. Ten thousand buildings, places of worship, schools, hospitals, bridges, and parks—all hammered into oblivion. Streets were so covered with debris, Vladka and Ben had to walk their bikes.

Destroying Warsaw had not served any military purpose. It had been done solely as an act of reprisal by Nazis against their so-called enemies, the Polish people.

Chapter 21

AMERICA

As they made their way through the rubble of Warsaw, Vladka felt no joy being back in the city where she'd grown up, even though her childhood years had been happy. She felt no relief over the war having ended. If she felt anything at all, it was loneliness and sadness, seeing around her an open grave of 350,000 Jews.

Within a week of their return to Warsaw, Vladka and Ben received news that Ben's parents were alive and staying near the cemetery toolshed that had been their home in hiding. Against all odds, Ben and his family were reunited. He located a house where his parents and sister could at last live in the open, without hiding, for the first time in years.

This entire time, Vladka had worn the ring Ben's mother had given her. Even though Vladka and Ben considered themselves married, they had had no chance for a real wedding, and Ben's parents insisted they have a proper Jewish ceremony. In February 1945, in Ben's parents' new home, surrounded by a small crowd of other recently liberated Jews, Vladka and Ben were married in what was rumored to be the first Jewish wedding since the liberation of Warsaw.

Vladka and Ben could envision no future for themselves in postwar Poland. The war was over, but not the antisemitism. Instead, they decided to immigrate with Ben's family to America as soon as possible. After a short stay in the Polish city of Łódź, which had been spared the Nazi bombings, the entire family hitched a ride on a freight truck and eventually arrived in the American zone of liberation in Munich, Germany. After much effort and waiting, they were able to board the SS *Marine Flasher*, one of the first refugee ships to leave war-torn Europe.

Vladka, Ben, and Ben's family arrived in New York City on May 24, 1946, along with other DPs, "Displaced Persons"—people who no longer had a home in Europe after the war. They had no luggage and no money. All that remained from a life that defied description were cold, tragic memories.

Life was very difficult for Vladka and Ben when they first arrived in America. Seeing a policeman or anyone in uniform filled them with fear. Hearing a telephone ring triggered attacks of anxiety. When they rented their first apartment, they felt compelled to build a hiding place. They ate quickly, as they had during the Nazi era, never knowing when the next roundup would come or when they would have food again. The brightest events in those postwar years were when Vladka gave birth to two children, Steven and Ana. When they grew up, both children became doctors and had families of their own. Those were moments Vladka and Ben cherished beyond description.

Apart from these few facts, however, not much is known about Vladka's early life in America. According to her son, Steven, this was a conscious decision on her part as she did not feel that such personal details were important to share. "I'm just one person who managed to survive out of so many millions who were killed in ghettos, in camps, in mass shootings," she said. What mattered, in her opinion, was bearing witness to the history of the Jewish people during the Holocaust.

Even when she agreed to explain what she went through, Vladka doubted anyone could possibly understand. Once, in an interview, she attempted to describe her terror as Germans came to deport her and banged loudly on her door. The journalist asked, "Why didn't you just refuse to open the door?"

Vladka shook her head. "The journalist was thinking with her normal mind about things in normal times," she later explained. "It was impossible for her to grasp what life was like in those *un*-normal times when Nazis just kicked down doors and killed everyone inside.

"Even today, so many years later," she continued, "I don't think scholars or historians can actually understand what it was like, or what total destruction looks like. So many young people were murdered, including one-and-a-half million Jewish children. Who can say what they might have achieved had they lived, what kinds of contributions they would have made to the world?

"I get the feeling people think I'm some kind of hero," she went on, "that I did 'big' things. I don't see it like that. We didn't think of ourselves as heroes. We didn't have a choice. We were doing what needed to be done, responding to what the Germans were doing to us. People who talk about survivors as heroes are seeing with today's eyes, not the eyes of someone who was there. We can't claim that we did something special. Everyone faced the same dangers. Everyone had the same odds of dying.

"Survival," she said, "was an accident."

Vladka and Ben Meed shortly after the war.

Chapter 22

TEACHING TEACHERS

Eventually, Vladka wrote a memoir about her experiences and the experiences of other Jews in Warsaw during the war. She called it *On Both Sides of the Wall*. It was published in Yiddish in 1948 and in English in 1993.

Vladka wanted to tell the story not just of the killings, which had no parallel in human history—killings in gas chambers, killings by torture—but also the story of life, the life of the Jewish people as it had been lived before the war: the traditions, the holidays, the families, the love. She wanted to tell that story, especially to young people. That eventually led her to start a program for teachers.

"Teachers need to know the story themselves before they can tell it to their students," she explained. "I started with maybe thirty teachers. We brought them to Israel to learn about the Holocaust, not because we didn't have scholars in the United States, but because I felt it was important for teachers to be close to the Jewish people. I wanted them to see the continuity of the Jewish people after the disaster of the Holocaust, how life has been established again by those who survived.

"I thought being in Israel might also help teachers understand why Jews are so proud of their nation. The Holocaust happened to the Jewish people when there was no Israel, when we did not have our own country, our own army, and when the doors of all the other countries were closed to us.

"This is not ancient history," Vladka said. "Even today, all it would take for the horror to happen again is a small group that wants to again spread the disease of hatred and make other people think like them. If we are going to prevent anything like this ever happening again, it will be by preparing young people to know that righteousness and evil both exist.

"The biggest danger," she cautioned, "is indifference to what happens to people around you. It was the world's indifference to what Hitler was doing that led to the murder of six million Jews and millions of other so-called 'enemies' of the Nazis. Many leaders around the world knew what was going on—this was Warsaw, in the middle of Europe, not some remote place—and the Jews were desperate for someone, some country, to come to their aid. Eventually help came, but too late for most of the Jews of Europe.

"Despite the tragedy that happened then, we are all part of the same world today," Vladka concluded. "We cannot live without other people. The world is filled with good people, and we should believe in their goodness. What I know now is that we also have to be alert to the evil."

EPILOGUE

In 1978, Vladka and Ben returned to Warsaw. They found a small Jewish community struggling to reassert itself in a country their ancestors had lived in for nearly a thousand years. As Vladka and Ben walked down the streets of their youth, they could not avoid a feeling of alienation. The street names were different, and the newly built concrete apartment blocks were flat and impersonal compared with the exquisite architecture of the city before the war. What had once been a vibrant world of Jewish commerce, education, and culture was now a line of nondescript office buildings, a few forlorn trees, and a handful of broken benches.

Not far from where they stood was the railroad siding where Jews had been transported to the death camp Treblinka. Now, in the middle of the block, there was a gas station—an ironic reminder of how death had come to nearly one million of Poland's Jews. On a low brick wall that flanked one end of the gas station, Vladka noticed a small plaque with a few sentences etched in Yiddish, Polish, and Hebrew.

THIS IS THE PLACE FROM

WHICH THE NAZIS SENT

TENS OF THOUSANDS OF JEWS TO THEIR DEATH.

There were no other plaques, memorials, or signage to indicate the place where a band of Jewish teenagers, with little more than their wits, had for nearly six weeks held off the formidable Nazi death machine. The experience reinforced for Vladka and Ben the importance of assuring that their story would always be remembered.

Vladka and Ben helped plan the 1981 World Gathering of Jewish Holocaust Survivors held in Israel, the first event of its kind. The American chapter of the gathering, held in Washington, DC, in 1983, attracted 20,000 survivors and their families. Ben served as president of the American Gathering until his death.

In the 1980s, Vladka and Ben also started the Registry of Jewish Holocaust Survivors, a worldwide database that allows Holocaust survivors and their families to search for relatives and friends. It now contains information on nearly 200,000 individuals and is housed at the United States Holocaust Memorial Museum in Washington, DC, of which Ben was a founding member.

Vladka died in 2012 at age ninety. Ben had died a few years before her at age eighty-eight. Together, they had formed an extraordinary, lifelong partnership that endured for nearly seventy years.

They are remembered for their unceasing dedication to keeping the memory of the Holocaust alive for future generations.

1979—Vladka and Ben Meed at the White House with United States president Jimmy Carter and Elie Wiesel, Holocaust survivor and author of *Night*.

Glossary

antisemitism—Hatred, hostility, or violence toward people because they are Jewish. Antisemitism may take the form of efforts to isolate, oppress, or otherwise injure Jewish people. Antisemitism also includes promoting prejudiced or negative stereotypes about Jews.

Aryan—The word "Aryan" comes from the ancient Sanskrit language and means "noble." The Nazi Party promoted the false notion that the German people were the "noble master race" and thus superior to Jews, Black people, Roma (gypsies), and others whom they deemed "inferior," based on bizarre, made-up ideas of race, heredity, and biology.

black market—The German authorities severely restricted the amount of food that could be sold to Jews. Obtaining food through other ways became critical to survival. The black market was an area of the ghetto where food and other goods could be bought or bartered illegally. Because the market was illegal and not regulated, it also gave unethical people a chance to take advantage of the poor and hungry by charging them exorbitant prices.

comrade—A close friend, a companion who shares one's activities, or a fellow member of an organization.

curfew—A regulation requiring people to remain indoors between specified hours, typically at night.

Gentile—A non-Jewish person.

Gestapo— The Gestapo (Geheime Staatspolizei) were the Nazi secret police, empowered to wipe out any political opposition. At its peak in 1944, the Gestapo's active officers within Germany numbered 16,000, policing a population of 66 million. Yet their powers were unchecked, and the **SS** became the foremost enforcer of policy, at times acting as lawgiver, jury, and executioner all at once. One of the Gestapo's main responsibilities was coordinating the deportation and murder of Jews.

Hitler, Adolf—Hitler (1889–1945) was made chancellor of Germany in 1933 and promoted the made-up idea of a biologically superior Aryan, or Germanic, master race of strong, tall, blond-haired, blue-eyed ideal humans. To rouse the German people to his concocted beliefs, Hitler focused his propaganda against Jews, whom he declared were responsible for all of Germany's domestic problems. The solution he implemented to these problems—referred to as "the final solution"—was to exterminate the entire Jewish population of Europe. Documents discovered after the war indicate that, had Hitler won the war, he would have extended his plan to include the murder of all Jews on Earth. After being informed that his army had surrendered, and following the Nazi principle of "death before dishonor," Hitler committed suicide in a Berlin bunker.

Holocaust—The word "holocaust" comes from the Greek language and means "burnt offering." The Holocaust refers to the systematic, state-sponsored murder of some six million Jews by Nazi Germany and its allies.

Jewish police—Mainly men, although also a few women, who thought that by cooperating with the Nazis, they and their families would be immune from deportation. The Germans forced the Jewish police to carry out their orders so the Germans wouldn't always have to deal directly with Jews. An order might come to round up a number of Jews for deportation to Treblinka, and the Jewish police would be responsible for finding that amount of Jews and bringing them in for deportation. The Jewish police usually knew where Jews were hiding and used wooden batons to beat them into the open and onto trucks that took them to the trains.

Molotov cocktails—An improvised hand-thrown incendiary weapon, made by filling a container such as a bottle with a flammable liquid—for instance, gasoline—and inserting a piece of cloth that serves as the fuse. The fuse attached to the container is lit and the weapon is thrown, shattering on impact. This ignites the flammable liquid contained in the bottle and spreads flames.

Nazis—Members or supporters of Germany's National Socialist German Workers' (Nazi) Party, which advocated extreme loyalty to their leader, Adolf Hitler; fanatical antisemitism; pseudoscientific racism; and the belief in the German people as the Aryan, or master race.

resistance—"Resistance," in the context of the Holocaust, refers to rising up against Nazi oppression. Continuing with religious observances, classes, artistic performances, and other actions forbidden by the Nazis was also considered a form of resistance.

SS—The SS (Schutzstaffel, or Protection Squads) was originally established as Adolf Hitler's personal bodyguard unit. Later, the SS became an elite guard, empowered to carry out all security-related duties without regard for legal restraint.

underground—The underground comprised various groups working to thwart the Nazi dictatorship by sabotaging German arms depots; blowing up bridges, trains, and offices; stealing weapons and food and smuggling them to resistance groups; and breaking prisoners out of Nazi jails. By the time of the Warsaw Ghetto Uprising, these various groups had more or less joined together as a united coalition.

Warsaw—Before World War II, Warsaw, the capital of Poland, was the largest center of Jewish educational and cultural activity. Of the city's 1.3 million residents, one-third (about 350,000) were Jews.

Yiddish—Yiddish is a language historically spoken by Jewish people from central and eastern Europe. A Germanic language that incorporates many words from Hebrew, Yiddish is today spoken mainly by some communities of religious Jews in the United States and Israel.

zloty—Zloty was the currency used in 1940s Poland. Zlotys were printed bank notes. In today's market, one zloty is worth about twenty US cents.

Acknowledgments

Those of us who attempt to tell the story of witnesses to the Holocaust have a responsibility to historic accuracy. Every time a life, an event, a detail of the Holocaust is misrepresented, it fuels the agenda of those who would deny that the Holocaust happened at all. Sadly, in recent years the number of deniers has grown.

Consequently, in telling the story of Vladka Meed, it was important to enlist the help of experts. I am indebted to Vladka and Ben's son, Dr. Steven Meed, for his encouragement and for his reassurance that the book is faithful to her voice.

For his review of historical details, I am grateful to Sam Kassow, the Charles H. Northam Professor of History at Trinity College (Hartford, CT). Among his many achievements, Professor Kassow was a consultant to the Museum of History of the Polish Jews, which opened on the site of the Warsaw Ghetto.

For his reading of the manuscript, I am equally indebted to Lawrence L. Langer, Alumnae Chair and Professor Emeritus of English at Simmons College, and a leading authority on Holocaust survivor testimony. He is the author of many distinguished books, most recently *The Afterdeath of the Holocaust* (2021).

Photo Credits

About the Author

Joshua M. Greene is an award-winning documentary filmmaker and the author of several acclaimed books, including *Signs of Survival: A Memoir of the Holocaust*, cowritten with Renee Hartman, and *My Survival: A Girl on Schindler's List*, cowritten with Rena Finder. A former instructor of Holocaust history at Hofstra and Fordham Universities, Joshua Greene sits on the Board of Advisors to the Fortunoff Video Archive for Holocaust Testimonials at Yale University. He lives in Old Westbury, New York.

TURN THE PAGE TO LEARN ABOUT
THREE OTHER POWERFUL TRUE
STORIES OF THE HOLOCAUST.

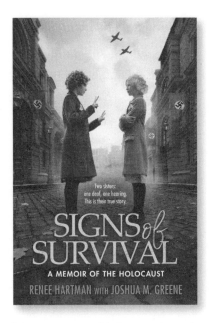

R ENEE: *I was ten years old then, and my sister was eight. The responsibility was on me to warn everyone when the soldiers were coming because my sister and both my parents were deaf.*

I was my family's ears.

As Jews living in 1940s Czechoslovakia, Renee, Herta, and their parents were in immediate danger when the Holocaust came to their door. Their parents were taken away, and the two sisters went on the run. Eventually, they, too, were captured and taken to the concentration camp Bergen-Belsen. Communicating in sign language and relying on each other for strength in the midst of illness, death, and starvation, Renee and Herta would have to fight to survive the darkest of times.

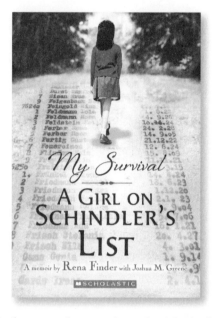

Rena Finder was eleven when the Nazis forced her and her family—along with all the other Jewish people of Krakow, Poland—into the ghetto. Then Rena and her mother ended up working for Oskar Schindler, a German businessman who employed Jewish prisoners in his factory. But Rena's nightmares were not over. She and her mother were deported to the concentration camp Auschwitz. With great cunning, it was Schindler who set out to help them escape.

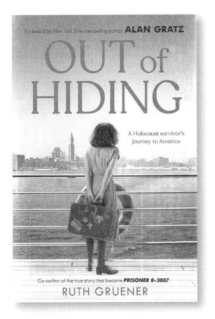

R uth Gruener was a hidden child during the Holocaust. At the end of the war, she and her parents were overjoyed to be free. But their struggles as displaced people had just begun.

In war-ravaged Europe, they waited for paperwork that would grant them a chance to come to America. Once they arrived in Brooklyn, Ruth started at a new school and tried to make friends—but she continued to fight nightmares and flashbacks of her time during World War II.

The family's perseverance is a classic story of the American dream, but it also illustrates the difficulties that millions of immigrants face in the aftermath of trauma.